ORGANIZATIONAL DYNAMICS:

Diagnosis and Intervention

ORGANIZATIONAL DYNAMICS:
Diagnosis and Intervention

JOHN P. KOTTER
Harvard University

ADDISON-WESLEY PUBLISHING COMPANY
Reading, Massachusetts • London • Amsterdam
Menlo Park, California • Don Mills, Ontario • Sydney

This book is in the Addison-Wesley Series:

ORGANIZATION DEVELOPMENT

Editors:
Edgar H. Schein
Richard Beckhard
Warren G. Bennis

ISBN 0-201-03890-0
ABCDEFGHIJK-DO-798

FOREWORD

It has been five years since the Addison-Wesley series on organization development published the books by Roeber, Galbraith, and Steele, and it is almost ten years since the series itself was launched in an effort to define the then-emerging field of organization development. Almost from its inception the series enjoyed a great success and helped to define what was then only a budding field of inquiry. Much has happened in the last ten years. There are now dozens of textbooks and readers on OD; research results are beginning to accumulate on what kinds of OD approaches have what effects; educational programs on planned change and OD are growing; and there are regional, national, and even international associations of practitioners of planned change and OD. All of these trends suggest that this area of practice has taken hold and found an important niche for itself in the applied social sciences and that its intellectual underpinnings are increasingly solidifying.

One of the most important trends we have observed in the last five years is the connecting of the field of planned change and OD to the mainstream of organization theory, organizational psychology, and organizational sociology. Although the field has its roots primarily in these underlying disciplines, it is only in recent years that basic textbooks in "organization behavior" have begun routinely referring to organization development as an applied area that students and managers alike must be aware of.

The editors of this series have attempted to keep an open mind on the question of when the series has fulfilled its function and should be allowed to die. The series should be kept alive only as long as new areas of knowledge and practice central to organization development are emerging. During the last year or so, several such areas have been defined, leading to the decision to continue the series.

On the applied side, it is clear that information is a basic nutrient for any kind of valid change process. Hence, a book on data gathering, surveys, and feedback methods is very timely. Nadler has done an especially important service in this area in focusing on the variety of methods that can be used in gathering information and feeding it back to clients. The book is eclectic in its approach, reflecting the fact that there are many ways to gather information, many kinds to be gathered, and many approaches to the feedback process to reflect the particular goals of the change program.

Team building and the appropriate use of groups continues to be a second key ingredient of most change programs. So far no single book in the field has dealt explicitly enough with this important process. Dyer's approach will help the manager to diagnose when to use and not to use groups and, most important, how to carry out team building when that kind of intervention is appropriate.

One of the most important new developments in the area of planned change is the conceptualizing of how to work with large systems to initiate and sustain change over time. The key to this success is "transition management," a stage or process frequently referred to in change theories, but never explored systematically from both a theoretical and practical point of view. Beckhard and Harris present a model that will help the manager to think about this crucial area. In addition, they provide a set of diagnostic and action tools that will enable the change manager in large systems to get a concrete handle on transition management.

The area of organization design has grown in importance as organizations have become more complex. Davis and Lawrence provide a concise and definitive analysis of that particularly elusive organization design—the matrix organization—and elucidate clearly its forms, functions, and modes of operation.

Problems of organization design and organization development are especially important in the rapidly growing form of organization known as the "multinational." Heenan and Perlmutter have worked in a variety of such organizations and review some fascinating cases as well as provide relevant theory for how to think about the design and development of such vastly more complex systems.

As organizations become more complex, managers need help in diagnosing what is going on both internally and externally. Most OD books put a heavy emphasis on diagnosing but few have provided workable schemes for managers to think through the multiple diagnostic issues that face them. Kotter has presented a simple and workable model that can lead the manager through a systematic diagnostic process while revealing the inherent complexity of organizations and the multiple interdependencies that exist within them.

Human resource planning and career development has become an increasingly important element in the total planning of organization improvement programs. Schein's book provides a broad overview of this field from the points of view of the individual and the total life cycle, the interaction between the career and other aspects of life such as the family, and the manager attempting to design a total human resource planning and development system.

The study of human resources in organizations has revealed the variety of new life-styles and value patterns that employees of today display, forcing organizations to rethink carefully how they structure work and what they consider to be "normal" work patterns. Cohen and Gadon provide an excellent review of various alternative work patterns that have sprung up in the last decade and are revolutionizing the whole concept of a normal workweek.

It is exciting to see our field develop, expand, strengthen its roots, and grow outward in many new directions. I believe that the core theory or the integrative framework is not yet at hand, but that the varied activities of the theoreticians, researchers, and practitioners of planned change and OD are increasingly relevant not only to the change manager, but also to line managers at all levels. As the recognition grows that part of *every* manager's job is to plan, initiate, and manage change, so will the relevance of concepts and methods in this area come to be seen as integral to the management process itself. It continues to be the goal of this series to provide such relevant concepts and methods to managers. I hope we have succeeded in some measure in this new series of books.

Cambridge, Massachusetts   Edgar H. Schein
March 1978

PREFACE

During 1974 and 1975 I conducted a clinical study of a highly diverse group of twenty-six organizations, including the following:

Financial

1 small bank
1 large trust company
1 medium-sized insurance company
1 small money management firm

Consumer products manufacturing

1 small jewelry company
1 moderate-sized shoemaker
1 small candy company

Other manufacturing

2 Fortune 500 companies
1 small instrumentation company

Business services

1 large consulting firm
1 medium-sized consulting firm
1 large advertising company

Retail

1 large clothing retailer
1 moderate-sized supermarket chain

Utilities

1 large electric utility

Communications

1 large newspaper
1 large communications company

Public

1 large city department
1 small state department
1 small federal agency

Health

1 large hospital

Education

1 small college
1 large college

Other nonprofit

1 small arts organization
1 communications organization

Data collection in the study consisted primarily of acquiring written information on each of these organizations and interviewing their top managers and a number of other well-informed insiders and outsiders. This book is one of a number of manuscripts that have evolved primarily from this research effort.

Numerous people contributed useful ideas during the development of this book, including Leonard Schlesinger, Ed Schein, Paul Lawrence, Chuck Gibson, Vijay Sathe, Connie Bourke, Anil Gupta, Joe Seher, Alan Frohman, Phelps Tracy, Victor Faux, Frank Leonard, Mike McCaskey, Chuck Christenson, Richard Beckhard, and Richard Boyatzis. Without their help, the cooperation of the heads of those twenty-six organizations, and the financial support of the Division of Research at Harvard Business School, this book would not have been possible.

Boston, Massachusetts   J. P. K.
April 1978

CONTENTS

1
INTRODUCTION

The past twenty-five years have witnessed the development of a number of tools or methods for improving organizational effectiveness that are based on behavioral science. These include, for example:

1. Management training techniques, such as Kepner-Trego clinics,[1] managerial grid sessions,[2] T-groups,[3] achievement motivation training,[4] and power motivation training[5]

---

1. Kepner-Trego Inc., Princeton, N. J., problem-solving and decision-making classes.
2. R. R. Blake and J. S. Mouton, *Building a Dynamic Corporation through Grid Organization Development* (Reading, Mass.: Addison-Wesley, 1969).
3. Chris Argyris, "T-Groups for Organizational Effectiveness," *Harvard Business Review* (March–April 1964): 84–97.
4. J. Aronoff and G. Litwin, "Achievement Motivation Training and Executive Advancement," *The Journal of Applied Behavioral Science* 7, (1971): 215.
5. D. C. McClelland, M. Rhinesmith, and K. Kristenen, "The Effects of Power Training for Staffs of Community Action Agencies." *The Journal of Applied Behavioral Science* 11, (1975): 92.

2. Methods of resolving conflict and improving relationships in organizations, such as team building,[6] intergroup labs,[7] confrontation meetings,[8] and third-party consultations[9]

3. Methods for more effectively designing formal organizational structure,[10,11] spatial arrangements,[12] pay systems,[13,14] jobs,[15,16] and performance appraisal systems[17]

4. Methods for measuring the current state of employee attitudes,[18] small group functioning,[19] organizational climate,[20] and organizational processes[21]

5. Broad approaches to the helping or intervention process, such as process consultation,[22] and survey feedback[23]

6. W. G. Dyer, *Team Building: Issues and Alternatives* (Reading, Mass.: Addison-Wesley, 1977).

7. R. R. Blake, H. A. Shepard, and J. S. Mouton, *Managing Intergroup Conflict in Industry* (Houston, Tex.: Gulf, 1964).

8. R. Beckhard, "The Confrontation Meeting," *Harvard Business Review* (March–April 1967): 45.

9. R. Walton, *Interpersonal Peacemaking: Confrontations and Third Party Consulting* (Reading, Mass.: Addison-Wesley, 1969).

10. J. R. Galbraith, *Designing Complex Organizations* (Reading, Mass.: Addison-Wesley, 1973).

11. P. R. Lawrence and J. W. Lorsch, *Organization and Environment* (Boston, Mass.: Division of Research, Harvard Business School, 1967).

12. F. I. Steele, *Physical Settings and Organizational Development* (Reading, Mass.: Addison-Wesley, 1973).

13. E. E. Lawler, II, *Pay and Organizational Effectiveness: A Psychological View* (New York: McGraw-Hill, 1971).

14. F. G. Lesieur, ed., *The Scanlon Plan: A Frontier in Labor-Management Cooperation* (Cambridge, Mass.: MIT, Industrial Relations Section, 1958).

15. L. E. Davis and R. Werling, "Job Design Factors," *Occupational Psychology* 34 (1960): 109–132.

16. W. J. Paul, K. B. Robertson, and F. L. Hertzberg, "Job Enrichment Pays Off," *Harvard Business Review* (March–April 1969): 61–78.

17. H. H. Meyer, E. Kay, and J. R. P. French, "Split Roles in Performance Appraisal," *Harvard Business Review* (Jan.–Feb. 1965): 123–129.

18. M. E. Shaw and J. M. Wright, *Scales for the Measurement of Attitudes* (New York: McGraw-Hill, 1967).

During this same twenty-five-year period, operations researchers, management scientists, financial and marketing specialists, and other nonbehavioral scientists also developed dozens of other tools to improve organizational functioning. These include production scheduling tools,[24] strategic planning tools,[25] financial control tools,[26] and market research tools,[27] to name only a few.

As a result of these developments, managers today have at their disposal an abundance of sophisticated tools that are potentially useful in helping them maintain or increase organizational effectiveness.[28] And the number of these techniques continues to increase each year.

This book has been written both for managers and for those specialists who help managers use organizational improvement tools. The book's objective is not, however, to provide another specific tool. Instead, it offers an integrative perspective on organizational dynamics that can help both managers and specialists to better decide when, where, and how to use (or not use) the ever-increasing number

19. J. K. Hemphill, *Group Dimensions: A Manual for Their Measurement*, Monograph 87 (Columbus: Ohio State University, Bureau of Business Research, 1956).

20. G. H. Litwin and R. A. Stringer, *Motivation and Organizational Climate* (Boston, Mass.: Harvard Business School, Division of Research, 1968).

21. R. Likert, *The Human Organization: Its Management and Value* (New York: McGraw-Hill, 1967).

22. E. H. Schein, *Process Consultation: Its Role in Organization Development* (Reading, Mass.: Addison-Wesley, 1969).

23. D. A. Nadler, *Feedback and Organizational Development: Using Data Based Methods* (Reading, Mass.: Addison-Wesley, 1977).

24. E. S. Buffa, *Production—Inventory Systems: Planning and Control* (Homewood, Ill.: Richard D. Irwin, 1968).

25. R. L. Ackoff, *A Concept of Corporate Planning* (New York: John Wiley, 1970).

26. J. C. Van Horne, *Financial Management and Policy* (Englewood Cliffs, N. J.: Prentice-Hall, 1968).

27. P. E. Green and D. S. Tull, *Research for Marketing Decisions* (Englewood Cliffs, N. J.: Prentice-Hall, 1975).

28. I say "potentially" because very little research exists that clearly documents the effectiveness of these tools.

of behavioral science and other organizational improvement techniques.

This introductory chapter will first attempt to demonstrate why such a perspective is needed. It will conclude by briefly describing how the book meets that need.

ORGANIZATIONAL IMPROVEMENT

The utilization of organizational improvement techniques generally requires the expenditure of some scarce resources. Just one team-building experience for a group of middle managers, for example, could easily cost an organization $2,500 or more.[29] Because of this fact, and because of the large number of tools and techniques that have been developed over the past few decades, managers today have far more options for improving their organization's effectiveness than they have resources. Even in the richest or most profitable organizations, most managers will be able to afford (in the short run) to use only a very limited number of the potential methods, even if they believe very strongly in investing resources in organizational improvement.

At the same time, today's managers are also faced with a general situation that has been continuously becoming more complex. Their organizations grow, develop new products, offer new services, incorporate additional technologies, and have a more heterogeneous work force. They often must cope with more sophisticated competitors, increasingly international operations, and more governmental interventions. This complexity often makes it less and less obvious how healthy or sick their organizations actually are. It also makes it less obvious how important various known problems are, and what the second- and third-order consequences of some set of actions—such as the use of some organizational development tool—will be.

Because of the complexity of contemporary organizations and the proliferation of organizational improvement tools, managers are

---

29. This estimate is based on the following assumptions: seven managers and one facilitator; a two-day session; average manager's time cost $150/day; facilities cost $100.

forced to make very difficult resource allocation decisions when they consider organizational improvement issues. For example, a manager who is considering bringing in an OD consultant, or using an employee attitude survey, or team building on a large scale, will often have great difficulty answering questions like the following:

1. Does this use of limited resources really make sense? What are the risks? Exactly how will it help my organization's effectiveness? How much will it help? Exactly what are the second-order consequences of this decision?

2. Could I better use these limited resources in another way? If I were to use the same amount of money to increase our advertising, would orders improve enough to ease the tensions around here and eliminate the problems we are currently experiencing?

3. Is this the proper time to use this tool (or method or approach)? Might it not make more sense to wait a month, a year, or even longer? How will its impact differ if done today rather than a year from now?

Managers will sometimes turn to specialists, such as OD professionals, to help them answer such questions. Sometimes these specialists can and do help, but often they too are unable to articulate convincing answers.

The consequences of this situation are predictable. Since they lack confidence in their assessment of the risks and benefits of organizational improvement techniques, managers quite often choose not to use them. As a result, many potentially useful techniques are seriously underutilized. Even when they are used, they are sometimes used inappropriately. Managers select the wrong techniques, or use them at the wrong time or in the wrong way. Then, when their expectations are not fulfilled, they tend to become even less willing to experiment with organizational improvement tools.

It is, of course, impossible to calculate the human and economic costs of either misusing organizational improvement tools or underutilizing them. But from my own observations over the past few years, I suspect the cost is very significant.

THE BOOK'S PURPOSE

This book has been written to provide both managers and organizational improvement specialists with a useful way of thinking about organizational improvement issues. It presents an integrative model of organizational dynamics that can help them answer the difficult questions they need to raise when assessing organizational health, selecting improvement tools, and implementing their choices.

The model of organizational dynamics presented in this book draws its ideas from a broad range of specialized work. It attempts to integrate concepts and findings across the many fragmented and often competing "camps" in which organization theory has been developed over the past few decades. The most important of these competing camps of ideas include:

1. Organizational sociology versus organizational psychology versus economics versus the various management disciplines versus political science versus organizational behavior

2. Natural systems theories versus rational-cybernetic theories[30]

3. Theories of manufacturing organizations versus profit-making service organizations versus public organizations versus nonprofit organizations, and so on[31]

---

30. The natural systems perspective is rooted in the work of Mayo, Roethlisberger, and Barnard. See, for example, *Management and The Worker*, by F. J. Roethlisberger, and W. J. Dickson (Cambridge, Mass.: Harvard University Press, 1939) and *The Functions of the Executive* by C. Barnard (Cambridge, Mass.: Harvard University Press, 1938). The rational systems perspective, on the other hand, comes from Taylor, L. Gulick and L. Urwick, and even M. Weber. See, for example, *Papers on the Science Administration* by L. Gulick and L. Urwick (New York: Augustus M. Kelley Publishers, 1969). More recently, this rational systems perspective has evolved into a "rational-cybernetic" perspective as the result of works such as W. R. Ashby's *Design for a Brain* (London, England: Chapman & Hall, 1952).

31. Fully one-third of J. G. March's *Handbook of Organizations* (Chicago: Rand-McNally, 1969) focuses on specific types of organizations (e.g., unions, businesses, hospitals, etc.). In addition, many of the more interesting theories of organizational behavior are really theories of a subclass of organizations, because they were created from or tested with data from only a subclass.

4. Theories of "process" versus theories of "structure"[32]

5. Theories with "cause and effect" relationships among system elements versus theories with "association"-based relationships[33]

6. "One best way" theories versus "contingency" theories[34]

All of these camps have contributed some ideas and concepts that shed light on organizational dynamics. The model presented in this book attempts to reconcile and integrate these ideas into a perspective that can be helpful to both managers and organizational improvement specialists.

The analytical framework, a model, is presented in the next four chapters. Chapter 2 begins the explanation by describing the major conceptual elements in the model, while Chapters 3–5 focus on the dynamic interaction of those elements. Chapter 6 discusses implications regarding organizational effectiveness and barriers to effective organizational development. Chapter 7 gives a number of specific examples of how managers and organizational specialists can use the model to help them with their work. Finally, Appendix A consolidates and summarizes questions developed throughout the book that can guide effective organizational diagnosis and intervention.

---

32. For example, Richard Hall's excellent review of organization theory and research divides the subject matter into four parts: the nature of organization; organizational structure; internal organizational processes; and organizations and society. See *Organizations: Structure and Process* (Englewood Cliffs, N. J.: Prentice-Hall, 1972).

33. For example, some major works like March and Simon's *Organizations* (New York: John Wiley, 1958) and D. Katz and R. L. Kahn's *The Social Psychology of Management* (New York: John Wiley, 1966) focus mostly on cause-and-effect relationships, while others such as J. Woodward's *Industrial Organization: Theory and Practice* (New York: Oxford University Press, 1965) focus on correlations and associations.

34. Much of organization theory has developed either from the point of view that some types of organizational behavior are always "best" (such as R. Likert, *The Human Organization* (New York: McGraw-Hill, 1967) or from the point of view that what is effective or best depends (or is contingent) on numerous factors (such as P. Lawrence and J. Lorsch, *Organization and Environment* (Boston: Harvard Business School, 1967).

2
THE MAJOR CONCEPTUAL ELEMENTS

The model of organizational dynamics described in this book is made up of seven major elements[1]:

1. Key organizational processes

2. The external environment

3. Employees and other tangible assets

4. Formal organizational arrangements

5. The internal social system

6. The organization's technology

7. The dominant coalition.

The purpose of this chapter is simply to define and briefly discuss these seven elements. Little effort will be made to show how they

---

1. My criteria for selecting the major elements included in the model were that (a) there should be convincing evidence in the existing literature that each is an important factor in understanding organizational dynamics; (b) they should be as mutually exclusive and collectively exhaustive as possible; and (c) they all should be helpful in explaining the dynamic evolution of those real organizations with which I am thoroughly acquainted.

interact, or what leads to organizational effectiveness or ineffectiveness. Subsequent chapters will focus on these other issues.

KEY ORGANIZATIONAL PROCESSES

The first, and central, element in this model focuses on two interdependent sets of processes, one of which involves matter and/or energy, the other information.[2] Specifically, these key organizational processes can be defined as the major information-gathering, communication, decision-making, matter/energy-transporting, and matter/energy-converting actions of the organization's employees and machines.[3] There are many such processes in organizations, and they are usually labeled according to their purpose—such as the purchasing process, the market-planning process, the leadership process, or the product X production process. Taken together, these processes make up what many people would refer to as the *behavior* of a formal organization.

All organizations import, convert, and export a variety of types of information and matter/energy. These processes are of central importance because, as in other living systems, survival and growth requires that more matter/energy be imported than exported. That is, survival depends on an organization's ability to establish a "favorable" set of exchanges with some external environment. And while luck certainly plays some role in creating and maintaining a favorable exchange, in most formal organizations the key to generating matter/energy surplus lies in information processes. Most formal orga-

---

2. James Miller and others have argued convincingly that there are two fundamental processes in organizations, as stated. A variety of social scientists have studied either the information or the energy/matter processes, although not many have studied both. A large number of "structuralists" have ignored both, choosing instead one or more of the other elements in this model.

3. For a review of the literature on information and matter/energy processes see Chapter 12 in P. Khandwalla, *The Design of Organizations* (New York: Harcourt Brace Jovanovich, 1977), and J. Miller, "Living Systems: The Organization" *Behavioral Science* **17** (1972): 1–182.

Table 2.1

Relevant Questions in Determining the Present State of an Organization's
Key Processes

1. What supplies (matter/energy resources) does the organization import? In what volume? At what cost?

2. Exactly how are these resources transported and converted into goods or services?

3. How are the goods or services disposed of? In what volume?

4. What other processes exist to manage the processes in questions 1-3 and to plan for the future?

5. How efficient are these processes (in questions 1-4)? How much matter/energy is unnecessarily wasted?

6. On the basis of answers to questions 1-4, what are the key decisions made in the organization?

7. How are these decisions made? That is,
   a) What individual or group makes these decisions?
   b) Exactly how does the individual or group make these decisions?
   c) What information is used?
   d) Where does that information come from?

8. How rational are these decisions? How effective are the various decision-making processes?

nizations survive because their employees and machines gather and process information to help them make decisions about the matter/energy they import, convert, and export, in order to create a matter/energy surplus (input/output) that at a minimum will allow the organization to survive.

These key processes can be found in a fairly wide variety of states in contemporary organizations. In some organizations the processes are much more elaborate, differentiated, and complex than in others; a small firm might not even have an identifiable market research process, for example, while a large organization might have a number of different ones. In some organizations certain types of processes might be much more important than in other organizations; in a consulting firm, for example, information processes might predominate, while in a steel-manufacturing firm, matter/energy processes might be most numerous. Certainly in some organizations the expenditure of matter/energy is much more efficient than in other organizations. And in some, the decision-making processes are much more effective at creating an input/output surplus.

To determine the state of a specific organization's key processes, one needs essentially to trace the flow of both matter/energy and information into, through, and out of an organization. This requires finding answers to questions like those shown in Table 2.1.

THE EXTERNAL ENVIRONMENT

The second major element in this model is an organization's *external environment,* which is made up of two basic parts: the task environment and the wider environment. An organization's *task environment* can be defined as *all possible suppliers (of labor, information, money, materials, and so on), markets, competitors, regulators, and associations that are relevant in light of the organization's current products and services.* This, then, represents an organization's immediately relevant external environment. The *wider environment* is a residual environment that can be defined by such indicators as *public attitudes, the state of technological development, the economy, the occupational system, the political system, the demographic characteristics of people and organizations, the society's social structure, current price levels, laws, and so on.*[4]

Economists originally and, in the past decade, organization theorists have clearly demonstrated that to understand an organization's internal processes one needs to understand its environment.[5]

---

4. For a review of the external environment literature, see W. Starbuck, "Organizations and Their Environments" in Dunnette's *Handbook of Industrial and Organizational Psychology* (Chicago: Rand McNally, 1976) and Chapter 10 in Richard Hall, *Organizations* (Englewood Cliffs, N. J.: Prentice-Hall, 1972).
5. Psychologists, in particular, still tend to ignore or diminish the importance of the external environment when studying organizations or advising managers.

Table 2.2
Relevant Questions in Determining the State of an Organization's External
Environment

---

1. Considering the organization's current products or services, what other organizations, groups, or important people constitute its task environment? That is, who are the relevant potential suppliers, customers or clients, regulators, competitors, and so on?

2. What are the key characteristics of the various entities in the task environment in terms of size, objectives or desires, stability, capabilities, technologies used, attitudes about the organization, and so on?

3. If the organization is in a clearly definable industry, and thus has competitors, why is it that some of its competitors are more successful than others? What are the key success factors in this industry?

4. With whom does the organization currently interact? How dependent is it on each of those external elements? In each case, what is the basis of that dependence? How much countervailing power does the organization have? What is the basis of that power?

5. What are the most important characteristics of the organization's outer environment? What are the current economic, political, legal, technological, and social trends of importance?

Because organizations must rely on their environments for providing inputs and disposing of outputs, the number and size of competitors and suppliers, the diversity of the markets served, the characteristics of regulators and associations, the attitudes of the public at large toward the organization, and the rate at which these factors are changing can all be relevant forces that help shape organizational processes.

Although the wider environments of organizations in any single country can be very similar, contemporary organizations can be found with a diverse range of task environments. As one might suspect, similar "types" of organizations (for example, organizations of the same size that offer similar products) tend to have similar task environments.

To determine the current state of a specific organization's external environment, one needs to identify and describe potentially relevant suppliers, customers or clients, regulators, competitors, and the like, as well as the organization's current relationship with these entities. If the organization is in an identifiable industry, it can be very helpful also to identify those characteristics that differentiate the more from the less successful competitors in that industry (see Table 2.2).

EMPLOYEES AND OTHER TANGIBLE ASSETS

The third element in this model, which I shall call an organization's *employees and other tangible assets*, can be defined as *the size (or number) and internal characteristics of an organization's employees, plant and offices, equipment and tools, land, inventories, and money.*[6,7]

It is intuitively obvious to most people, I suspect, that the amount of resources an organization commands and the condition of these resources has a major effect on an organization's processes, and on its future development. An organization with ten employees simply cannot have the volume and diversity of processes than an organization with 100,000 employees can. The same is true for the firm with few physical assets compared with the firm with a billion dollars in assets. An organization with no engineering personnel will most likely be unable to establish the type of product development processes that a firm with engineering personnel can establish. An organization with one hundred employees who have many positive feelings about their jobs and company will probably be able to generate processes during a crisis period that a competitor with one hundred employees who have bad feelings about their jobs and company cannot generate.

Organizations can vary enormously in the makeup of their employees and other tangible assets. As one goes from the corner drug-

---

6. All organizational researchers to some degree take this element into account, perhaps because of its visibility: it is easy to see and obviously seems important. Nevertheless, nonpsychologists have by and large consistently treated human beings in an oversimplified manner and noneconomists have more often than not ignored or downplayed other assets that can often be treated mathematically.
7. For a review of the literature on the structure of individual personalities, see S. Maddi, *Personality Theories* (Georgetown, Ontario: Irwin-Dorsey, 1968) and Section III (pp. 469–644) in Dunnette's *Handbook of Industrial and Organizational Psychology* (Chicago: Rand McNally, 1976).

store to Litton Industries to the Roman Catholic Church, one sees gigantic variations in the amount of assets, their composition, their heterogeneity, and so on.

Determining the state of a specific organization's employees and other tangible assets requires that one inventory those assets (see Table 2.3). For nonhuman assets, it is important to determine their physical condition and their cash value. With human assets, it is important to identify not only their backgrounds and skills, but also their feelings about the organization, and their expectations about their future at work.

Table 2.3
Relevant Questions in Determining the Current State of an Organization's
Employees and Other Tangible Assets

---

1. What assets does the organization own, lease, or employ? Catalogue all the organization's owned or leased tangible assets, including land, buildings, equipment, supplies, inventories, cash, and securities. Also catalogue the number and types of people employed.

2. What condition are the nonhuman assets in? How well have they been maintained? How liquid are they? What price could each obtain if converted quickly into cash?

3. What are the backgrounds of different employee groups? What are their skills and abilities? How do they feel about the organization? What are their expectations regarding the organization and their future?

FORMAL ORGANIZATIONAL ARRANGEMENTS

The fourth element in this model is called *formal organizational arrangements,* and can be defined as *all formal systems that have been explicitly designed to regulate the actions of an organization's employees (and machines).* These formal arrangements would include structure (job design, departmentalization, a reporting hierarchy, rules and plans, teams and task forces) and operating systems

Table 2.4

Relevant Questions in Determining the Current State of an Organization's Formal Organizational Arrangements

1. What is the organization's formal structure? Draw a chart showing jobs, departmental groupings, a reporting hierarchy, responsibilities, and authorities. Also list any committees, teams, task forces, regular meetings, and so forth.

2. What types of formal procedures exist for the following:

   a) Allocating resources,
   b) Controlling financial resources,
   c) Measuring individual or unit performance,
   d) Selecting people,
   e) Training people,
   f) Rewarding people

(resource allocation systems, planning systems, measurement and reward systems, hiring and development systems).[8]

A great deal of research conducted in the past twenty years has confirmed what most practicing managers seem to have long recognized; formal arrangements can have an important impact on organizational dynamics.[9] Formal organizational structure, for example, typically influences employee behavior and organizational processes by specifying what individuals are responsible for, where in the organization they should work and with whom, what authority they have and to whom they are responsible, and how they should go about performing their tasks. Measurement systems influence behavior by gathering, aggregating, disseminating, and evaluating information on the activities of individuals or groups within the organization. Reward

---

8. Organizational, administrative, and management theorists, as well as sociologists, have usually explicitly dealt with formal organizational arrangements, although many have had a tendency to emphasize structure and ignore other subelements. Some psychologists, social psychologists, and economists seem to ignore formal arrangements altogether.

9. For a recent summary of our knowledge of formal arrangements, see J. P. Kotter *et al. Organizational Design and Change* (to be published in 1979); and J. R. Galbraith, *Organization Design* (Reading, Mass.: Addison-Wesley, 1977).

systems are usually designed to induce people to join an organization, and to work toward certain measured objectives. Selection and development systems have an impact on behavior by directly influencing the knowledge, skills, values, and personalities of employees.

Small and young organizations often have few formal systems, while older and large organizations usually have many. But the exact nature of the formal arrangements used can vary significantly even among large or small organizations. To determine the state of a specific organization's formal arrangements, analysts usually ask the kinds of questions shown in Table 2.4.

THE SOCIAL SYSTEM

The fifth element in this model, generally called the organization's *internal social system*, is made up of two main parts: culture and social structure. *Culture* can be defined as *those organizationally relevant norms and values shared by most employees (or subgroups of employees).* *Social structure* is defined as *the relationships that exist among employees in terms of such variables as power, affiliation, and trust.* [10]

Considerable evidence has been amassed since the now famous Hawthorne studies[11] that demonstrates the importance of this factor in organizational analysis.[12] Whenever people are brought together in sustained interaction, a social system emerges. This system of "informal" relationships, norms, and values then becomes another element that influences the behavior of those people. In an organization with a social system that places a high value on safety, for example, employees will tend to have ways of generating production processes that are different from those of employees in an organization whose social system does not value safety very much. A great deal of status

10. For one review of this literature, see Chapter 4, "The Social Structure of Work Groups," in P. Blau and W. R. Scott, *Formal Organizations* (San Francisco, Calif.: Chandler, 1962).
11. See F. J. Roethlisberger and W. J. Dickson, *Management and the Worker* (Cambridge, Mass.: Harvard University Press, 1939).
12. Nevertheless, economists and some of the better organization theorists essentially ignore this element.

Table 2.5

Relevant Questions in Determining the Current State of an Organization's Social System

---

1. What organizationally relevant norms exist among most employees or subgroups of employees? For example, what norms, if any, exist regarding how hard people should work and how conflicts among people should be resolved?

2. What organizationally relevant values exist among most employees or within subgroups of employees? Do any of those values relate to what the organization should be or should achieve?

3. What types of relationships exist among employees, especially regarding trust, level of cooperation, and power?

4. What types of relationships exist among natural subgroups in the organization, again regarding levels of cooperation, trust, and power?

---

stratification in the social system can make processing large amounts of complex information difficult and costly, whereas less status stratification can make it easier. Two organizations that are identical except for their employees' norms regarding "productivity" will generate different processes; the organization with high productivity norms will produce more. And so on.

As in the case of the other elements described so far, the internal social systems found among contemporary organizations can vary considerably. To determine the state of the social system in a specific organization, analysts tend to ask the kinds of questions shown in Table 2.5.

TECHNOLOGY

The sixth element in this model is the *organization's technology,* defined here as *the major techniques (and their underlying assumptions about cause and effect) that are used by an organization's employees while engaging in organizational processes, and that are programmed into its machines.* This is meant to be a rather broad definition of a term that is used with several meanings. This definition would include the craft of glass blowing, methods for doing market

Table 2.6

Relevant Questions in Determining the Current State of an Organization's
Technology

1. What is the organization's "core technology" (that method used in creating its primary goods or services)? Describe the technology—for example, if the organization is a manufacturing firm, does it use a job-shop, large-batch, mass-production, or process technology? How complex is it? What kind of assets are needed to use it?

2. What other technologies does the organization use to produce goods or services? Describe them.

3. What technologies does the organization use to administer itself? Describe these too.

research, and techniques for making steel. An important subpart of this element is what Thompson calls the core technology,[13] which might be defined as that technology (or technologies) associated with an organization's main product or service.[14]

Today, most economists and organization theorists seem to agree that technology plays a central role in shaping an organization's processes and its evolution over time.[15] Technology, much like employees and their tangible assets, influences the shape of an organization's processes by making some things feasible and some not. An organization that simply does not have a modern market research technology will tend to generate a market-planning process different from that of a similar firm having that technology. An organization whose core technology requires a large number of tasks to be completed sequentially will usually generate more complex coordination processes than an organization whose core technology allows tasks to be completed independently.

13. *Organizations in Action* (New York: McGraw-Hill, 1967).
14. For a discussion of current knowledge of "technology," see Chapter 3 in Charles Perrow, *Organizational Analysis* (Belmont, Calif.: Wadsworth, 1970) and Chapter 9 in Peter Drucker, *The Practice of Management* (New York: Harper & Row, 1954).
15. Yet many organizational psychologists, social psychologists, and management theorists essentially ignore this variable.

To determine the state of a specific organization's technologies, analysts consider the types of questions shown in Table 2.6. Answers to these questions can vary considerably: the differences between General Motors and the corner drugstore are striking. Indeed, one of the key components in creating the wide diversity that exists today in organizations is the development of many different production and administrative technologies since the beginning of the Industrial Revolution.

THE DOMINANT COALITION

The seventh and final element in this model is an organization's *dominant coalition,* defined as *the objectives and strategies (for the organization), the personal characteristics, and the internal relationships of that minimum group of cooperating employees who oversee the organization as a whole and control its basic policy making.*[16] As such, a dominant coalition could be as large as twenty people (or more) or, if no one is in control, as small as zero. While it is sometimes made up of the president (or director) and his or her lieutenants as designated by the formal structure, it sometimes excludes some of them and/or includes others.[17]

Virtually all people, I suspect, who have clinically studied formal organizations would agree that those who control an organization

---

16. Many management and leadership theorists have agreed on the importance of this element, but few organizational researchers have paid attention to it. Many of those who have examined an organization's leaders have focused only on the head of the organization or the executive committee, and not the dominant coalition. Some management theorists would probably give a larger role to the dominant coalition's, "business strategy." I have chosen not to, based on my own observation in fifty or more organizations and my reading of the empirically based literature on strategy.

17. For a review of relevant literature in this area see P. Khandwalla, *The Design of Organizations* (New York: Harcourt Brace Jovanovich, 1977), Chapters 10 and 11, and James Thompson, *Organizations in Action* (New York: McGraw-Hill, 1967).

Table 2.7
Relevant Questions in Determining the Current State of an Organization's
Dominant Coalition.

---

1. Who is in the organization's dominant coalition? Describe each of these people in terms of personal skills, attitudes, motives or desires, assumptions about how organizations should be organized and run, and so on.

2. What are the relationships among the members of the coalition? How cohesive a group is it? Who has the most power?

3. What goals and plans for the organization does the group share?

4. How powerful is this group vis-à-vis others in the organization? What is the basis of this power?

---

invariably leave their fingerprints on it. That is, the particular skills, interpersonal and cognitive orientations, goals and values of the dominant coalition influence an organization's processes in the same way that all employees influence the processes, only more so. Because the dominant coalition, by definition, occupies the top position of power in an organization's social system, it can have a larger overall impact than others who occupy lesser power positions.

Dominant coalitions in different organizations can vary considerably in their composition, like the other elements in this model. To determine the current state of an organization's dominant coalition, questions like those in Table 2.7 are useful.

SUMMARY AND DISCUSSION

The model of organizational dynamics presented in this book is made up of seven elements: a central "process" element, labeled key organizational processes, and six "structural" elements, labeled the external environment, employees and other tangible assets, formal organizational arrangements, the internal social system, the organization's technology, and the dominant coalition.[18] An appreciation for all of these elements is essential for people who are interested in organizational effectiveness.

This is not to say that to understand an organization, or to be able to help an organization improve its effectiveness, one needs comprehensive answers to all the questions in Tables 2.1–2.7. For all but the smallest of organizations, the amount of information required to thoroughly answer all of those questions is overwhelming. What is needed, instead, is a sensitivity to the potential relevance of each element, variable, or question highlighted in this model. This sensitivity, when combined with an understanding of how these elements and variables tend to interact, can be enormously helpful to both managers and organization specialists, especially those trained from a specialized point of view.

---

18. It is impossible to demonstrate (or prove) that these seven elements, defined as they are in this chapter, are the best way to conceptualize the parts of a system that focus on the dynamics of a formal organization. It is quite possible that one or two of the elements should be defined in a slightly different way, or perhaps that parts of the various elements should be reconceptualized and recombined into only six major elements. Nevertheless, the research on formal organizations does clearly suggest that all of the variables captured in the seven elements are potentially important in helping one to understand or predict organizational dynamics. Yet no other theory, framework, or model incorporates all of those variables.

3
SYSTEM DYNAMICS IN THE SHORT RUN

In order to understand how the seven elements described in Chapter 2 interact to create organizational dynamics, it is useful to distinguish among three time frames: the short run (hours to a few months), the moderate run (a few months to a few years), and the long run (a few years to a few decades). This chapter will examine system dynamics in a short-run time frame, and will focus on "cause-and-effect" relationships between the six structural elements and the organizational processes. Chapter 4 will discuss moderate-run dynamics, and will focus on the "alignment" or "fit" among the structural elements. Chapter 5 will then deal with long-run dynamics, and will introduce the additional concepts of "driving force" and "level of adaptability."

CAUSE-AND-EFFECT RELATIONSHIPS

In the short run, the most important relationships among the elements in this model are those of a cause-and-effect nature that connect the key organizational processes with the other elements. In a sense, the six *structural* elements provide the context in which the organizational *processes* emerge. At the same time, the processes have a continuous impact on all six other elements, which helps either to maintain or to change their states (see Fig. 3.1).

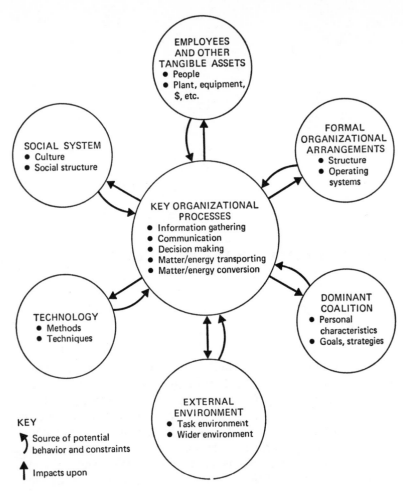

Fig. 3.1 Short-run dynamics.

To clarify the dynamics implicit in Fig. 3.1, consider the following brief description by a manager of organizational dynamics over a four-month period:

In April the demand for our new product line dropped considerably. With orders down, our deliveries began to decrease and our inventories began to increase. When top management became aware of this through the weekly operating reports, they did nothing at first. They hoped that their substantial marketing efforts, which were already in effect, would bring demand back to its previous level. But when orders continued at a very low level for six weeks, they decided to cut production way back and to lay off one hundred people. Within six weeks, inventories were down to normal again and orders for the new products were back in line with production. We didn't get hurt very much financially, but I think we lost some real credibility in the eyes of our production workers. Most of them had believed we wouldn't lay off a large number of people like that.

Within the framework shown in Fig. 3.1, these events can be broken down into eight discrete cause-and-effect-like actions (see Fig. 3.2). In some of these actions, a structural element has some clear effect on a key process: for example, the sequence of events begins with demand dropping in the external environment, which *causes* incoming orders to go down. In other actions, a key process has some effect on one or more of the structural elements: a reduced production process, for example, *causes* inventories to go down.

In order to understand or predict organizational dynamics in the short run, one needs to understand the two types of relationships that are present in Figs. 3.1 and 3.2. The first of these involves the shaping of the key organizational processes by the other six structural elements. The second type involves the impact of those processes on the six structural elements.

SHAPING THE ORGANIZATIONAL PROCESSES

Examples of influence relationships going from the six structural elements to the key organizational processes are shown in Table 3.1. Such relationships have been studied by a variety of social scientists. Economists, for example, have studied how the structure of the external environment shapes organizational processes (for example, "a monopolistic industry tends to cause inefficiency to emerge in organizational processes").[1] Social psychologists have studied how

---

1. See, for example, G. Stigler, *The Organization of Industry* (Homewood, Ill.: Irwin, 1968) and T. Marschek, "Theories of Economic Organization," in March's *Handbook of Organizations* (Chicago: Rand McNally, 1965).

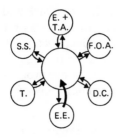

1. Demand from the external environment drops, causing incoming orders to go down.

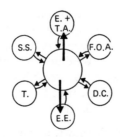

2. With the production process continuing at the same rate, the drop in orders causes deliveries to go down and shipments to inventory to go up.

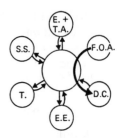

3. A formal control system maintains a process that causes top management to be alerted to these changes.

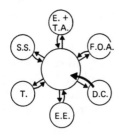

4. After watching the situation for a few weeks, top management intervenes in the process to slow production and reduce the work force.

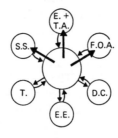

5. Their decisions are implemented—the production plan is changed, people are laid off, and the "no large layoff" belief is shattered.

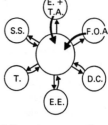

6. These changes cause the production process to slow.

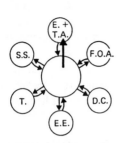

7. Shipments exceed production, causing inventories to go down.

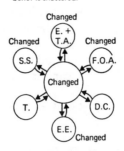

8. The system restabilizes with the states of five of the elements changed.

Fig. 3.2 An example of short-run cause and effect.

Table 3.1
Examples of How Each Structural Element
Might Influence the Key Processes in the Short Run

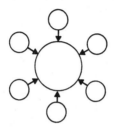

1. *External Environment.* A strike in the steel industry interupts the inflow of steel parts into the company's manufacturing processes.

2. *Dominant Coalition.* The president retires, and a very different type of individual is elected to succeed him, causing significant changes in the leadership processes within the company.

3. *Formal Arrangements.* A new compensation plan for salespeople creates a significant expansion of activity in the company's selling processes.

4. *Employees and Other Assets.* An increase in the educational level of the corporate financial staff causes an improvement in the quality of the financial analysis process.

5. *Internal Social System.* An increase in the level of trust between members of production and sales units causes a significant increase in information sharing for the new product development process.

6. *Technology.* The introduction of a new production control technology completely changes the nature of the production planning and control processes.

the social system shapes organizational processes (for example, "anti-company norms on the part of the work force tend to cause conflict and inefficiency to emerge in organizational processes").[2] Administrative theorists have focused on how formal organizational arrangements shape the processes (for example, "the installation of many rules and procedures tends to lead to more predictable and less flexible organizational processes").[3]

There are many conclusions one can draw from this type of research, a large number of which would be intuitively obvious to most managers and organizational specialists. But one particularly important conclusion is often not obvious to people. It can be stated as follows: The exact effect a structural element or a change in a structural element will have on an organization's key processes is a function not only of the prior states of the processes and that single element, but of the states of the other structural elements as well. Ignoring one or more of the structural elements can easily lead one to draw inaccurate conclusions regarding short-run dynamics.

For example, a management development executive once called in a consultant to help him evaluate why his company's management training program seemed to be having so little impact. In particular, the executive was concerned that programs aimed at generating more planning and performance evaluation processes did not seem to be very effective. After a review of the situation, the consultant found that the programs themselves were excellent; the problem was simply that the company's dominant coalition had not taken the programs, did not do much planning or performance evaluation themselves, and did not encourage others in the organization to plan or do performance evaluations. And their impact on the processes was far greater than that of two short training programs.

In this case, the executive was implicitly using a model of the situation that included only two elements—formal organizational arrangements and key organizational processes (see Fig. 3.3). On the

2. See, for example, J. Richard Hackman's "Group Influence on Individuals," in Dunnette's *Handbook of Industrial and Organizational Psychology* (Chicago: Rand McNally, 1976).
3. See, for example, J. R. Galbraith, *Organizational Design* (Reading, Mass.: Addison-Wesley, 1977).

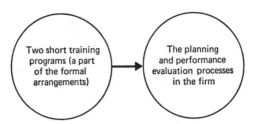

Fig. 3.3 An implicit model of short-run dynamics used by one executive.

basis of this model, he drew the logical conclusion that something must be wrong with the training programs if they were not causing a change in the firm's planning and performance evaluation processes. When the consultant helped him to think about his situation with the Fig. 3.1 model, he was able to see that there were alternative explanations as to why no change was occurring. By using the Fig. 3.1 model and by collecting additional data on employees, the social system, the dominant coalition, and so on, he concluded, as did the consultant, that the "problem" was not in the design of the training programs, but in the dominant coalition. On the basis of this new conclusion, he then temporarily stopped the ineffective training programs and focused his attention on the dominant coalition.

I have seen dozens of examples like this one in which managers or organization specialists misdiagnosed what was causing some type of short-run dynamic because they implicitly were using an inadequate model of the situation (like the one in Fig. 3.3). Basing their actions on that inaccurate diagnosis, they would then fail to create some type of a desired short-run change. Two of the most common types of failure can be characterized as follows:

1. Cases in which managers assume a process problem is being caused by one or more employees. The managers replace the employees, only to find that the problem remains or quickly reemerges. Often this occurs because the problem was in reality being caused by the internal social system, or the formal arrangements.

2. Cases in which applied behavioral scientists assume a process problem is being caused by the internal social system. They design and

implement interventions to change the social system, only to find that the problem does not disappear. In these cases, the problem is sometimes caused by the formal arrangements, sometimes by the technology being used, sometimes by the external environment, and sometimes by still other factors that the applied behavioral scientists initially ignored.

For example, the president of a high technology manufacturing firm once fired and replaced three directors of engineering in a period of just four years. In each case, he did so because the company's new product development process was not functioning well. He never really considered the possibility that other factors, some beyond the control of the engineering director, might be causing the problem. A subsequent diagnosis of this situation, by the corporate staff of the firm that acquired this manufacturing company, led to a very different conclusion. They decided that the process problems were being caused by a combination of factors, including some inappropriate informal norms, the lack of certain types of formal coordination arrangements, and some attitudes held by the key figure in the dominant coalition (the president). In support of their diagnosis, they found that the three former engineering directors were all pursuing successful careers elsewhere as heads of engineering in high technology manufacturing firms.

In another case, an internal staff organization specialist concluded that problems in her company's product shipping processes were being caused by the poor informal relations between key participants in that process—specifically some members of the sales force and the manufacturing department. Based on this conclusion, she designed and implemented a number of interventions aimed at improving those relationships in the social system. Immediately after her interventions, the shipping process improved somewhat. But this improvement lasted less than two months. Nine months later, when the company implemented a change in the definition of its task environment—it dropped one product and a set of customers, and added another product and customer group—the shipping process problem quickly disappeared and did not reemerge. After a post mortem of this affair, the same internal staff organization specialist drew two conclusions. First she decided that the process problem was primarily caused not by relations in the social system, but by a task environment that was making unrealistic demands on the organization. Second, she concluded that in the future she had better be more sensitive, while diagnosing the causes of process problems, to the effect of the task environment and other factors her training had not emphasized.

The basic lesson here is simple, but often not recognized: in thinking about how any single structural element shapes the key processes, it is critical that one consider the impact of the other elements too. Thinking in terms of simplified versions of Fig. 3.1 can be dangerous.

THE IMPACT ON THE STRUCTURAL ELEMENTS

Examples of possible influence relationships in the opposite direction, from the organizational processes to the structural elements, are shown in Table 3.2. Such relationships have been studied primarily by applied social scientists and practitioners. Indeed, the various "management" disciplines are all oriented toward shaping the organizational processes (that is, gathering information, making decisions, transporting and converting matter and energy) so as to have some impact on one of the structural elements in this model.[4] Advertising management, for example, is concerned with gathering information and making decisions that will have a certain impact on the attitudes and behaviors of an organization's customers. Production management deals with transporting and converting matter/energy so as to change raw materials into a finished product (tangible assets). Research and development management focuses on gathering information and making decisions to improve the firm's core technology. Public relations management focuses on information processing and decision making related to improving an organization's public image in its wider environment.

Once again, many of the conclusions one can draw from this type of research would be obvious to most managers and organization specialists. For example, virtually all of them would explicitly recognize

---

4. See, for example, P. Drucker, *Management* (New York: Harper & Row, 1976).

Table 3.2

Examples of How the Key Processes Can Influence Each of the Structural Elements in the Short Run

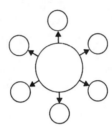

1. *External Environment.* A change in the advertising process causes demand for a certain product to increase 25 percent.

2. *Dominant Coalition.* A new reporting process for top management, which supplies them with more and different information about the firm's operations, causes their opinions about certain problems in the company to change considerably.

3. *Formal Arrangements.* A job evaluation process causes 10 percent of middle-level jobs to be redesigned.

4. *Employees and Other Tangible Assets.* When a great deal of bitter conflict emerges in one decision-making process, it immediately causes the job satisfaction of the people involved to go down.

5. *Internal Social System.* A new grievance process causes the relationships between workers and management to improve.

6. *Technology.* The research and development process causes the continuous expansion of the firm's core technology.

that in two or more different states, the organizational processes can expend significantly different amounts of matter/energy and yet still have the same impact on one of the structural elements (for example, two similar organizations can go about developing a new technology in very different ways, and both succeed, but at vastly different costs). But once again, some of the conclusions are not obvious to many people.

Just as was the case in thinking about how structural elements shape the key processes, managers will sometimes think of the impact key processes have on some structural elements in terms of models that do not include all the structural elements. For instance, in the example used at the start of this chapter, one wonders if the top managers involved recognized that the processes they created to change the production plan and lay off employees would also have an impact on the social system (shared beliefs about "no large layoff" were destroyed). If indeed they did not recognize those "unintended consequences," their mistake would hardly be unusual. This type of problem, especially involving an unintended impact on an internal social system, occurs frequently in organizations. Technically trained managers, in particular, often seem to ignore the possible impact of processes they generate on their internal social systems.

Younger managers and organization specialists, in particular, also often seem to underestimate the amount of energy that must be mobilized in a process in order to produce a change in some structural element in a short period of time. I personally have seen many examples in which people attempted to change an organization's formal structure, or to mold the attitudes of its customers, or to replace part of its dominant coalition, and in each case failed at least partially because they underestimated the energy needed to produce the change. In one case, for example, a relatively new staff manager identified some serious deficiencies in the skills and motivation of his company's two-hundred-person sales force. He designed a set of interventions to correct those deficiencies that called for most sales-people to go though two short (two-day) training courses over a six-month period, and to participate in some followup after the courses. His superiors gave their approval to his plan and he implemented it with the aid of one other staff member. Four months into the program, the staff manager began to realize just how difficult it was to produce the changes he desired, and how ineffective his small interventions were going to be. He concluded, for example, that some sales-people should probably not have been hired in the first place, and that some of the older sales-people would require considerable retraining before they would change habits developed over twenty to forty years. As a result, while completing the six-month program, he designed a more comprehensive two-year program. When he presented this new plan to his superiors, it was rejected. The feedback they had received from a disappointed sales management was that the first program had achieved very little. So they saw no reason to allocate more resources for more of the same. As such, the staff manager's unrealistic assumptions about how much energy would be required to produce a change not only led to an ineffective intervention, it also created a situation in which it would be even more difficult to produce that change in the future.

Of course, not all changes require considerable energy. But those changes in structures that are generally considered to be in a "positive" direction, from an organization's point of view, tend to require significant energy expenditure. As a result, it is quite possible for an organization to be in a position where it simply does not have the surplus matter/energy to make any number of changes that are ideally desired. To compete with Japanese manufacturers, for example, many analysts believe that United States steel makers need to make major changes in the technologies they use, in their physical assets, and in their dominant coalitions. Unfortunately, such changes, especially those requiring new plants and equipment similar to Japan's more modern production facilities, would cost far more money than the steel makers have available. How organizations get into such a position is an important issue that will be explored in later chapters.

SUMMARY AND DISCUSSION

The key system dynamics concerning the short run are of a cause-and-effect nature *between* the structural elements and the organizational processes. The six structural elements shape the key organizational processes. At the same time, the key processes continuously affect the structural elements in ways that help maintain or change their states. To predict an organization's behavior over a short period of time, one therefore needs (1) information on the states of the elements in the model and (2) an understanding of the two different types of cause-and-effect relationships involved (from social science and applied social science research). The better the information one has on the states of the elements, and the better one understands those cause-and-effect

Table 3.3
Relevant Questions for Understanding or Predicting Organizational
Dynamics in the Short Run

---

1. What is the current state of the following:

   a) The organization's key processes
   b) Its dominant coalition
   c) Its formal arrangements
   d) Its employees and other tangible assets
   e) Its social system
   f) Its technology
   g) Its external environment

2. What, if anything, is currently changing or might change in the near future?

3. Given your understanding of short-run cause and effect, how do you think each change would immediately affect the key processes (if it were a structural change) or each structural element (if it were a process change)?

4. What would be most likely to happen next? And then next? Trace the interaction of processes to structures to processes until the system achieves an equilibrium and stops changing, or at least for a period of time of three or four months.

---

relationships, the better one can account for and predict the system's behavior over short time periods (see Table 3.3).

While helpful in the short run, the cause-and-effect relationships discussed in this chapter are not very helpful in explaining past events or predicting future ones in a moderate to long-run time frame. To predict how an organization will evolve over a five-year period, for example, would require estimating and tracing hundreds of cause-and-effect interactions of the type shown in Fig. 3.2, and that is not very practical. To understand system dynamics from a moderate-run perspective, we have to move beyond cause-and-effect dynamics and examine the relationships among the six structural elements.

4
MODERATE-RUN DYNAMICS

Over moderate periods of time—let us say, from six months to six-years—organizations can obviously change much more than in the short run. This change can take almost an infinite number of paths and can appear, at least on the surface, more complex than the dynamics explored in the previous chapter, and more difficult to understand. Nevertheless, moderate-run dynamics display patterns that are just as comprehensible as short-run dynamics. They are simply different kinds of patterns.

Whereas the key to understanding short-run dynamics was the idea of cause-and-effect relationships between the structural elements and the key processes, the key to moderate-run dynamics lies in the relationships among the six structural elements in the model (Fig. 4.1), and in the concept of alignment.

ALIGNMENTS, NONALIGNMENTS, AND COALIGNMENT

As I have argued elsewhere,[1] some of the more interesting research and theory completed in the past two decades on formal organizations has focused on the relationships among two or more of the structural

---

1. See J. P. Kotter and P. R. Lawrence, *Mayors in Action* (New York: John Wiley, 1974), Chapter 13.

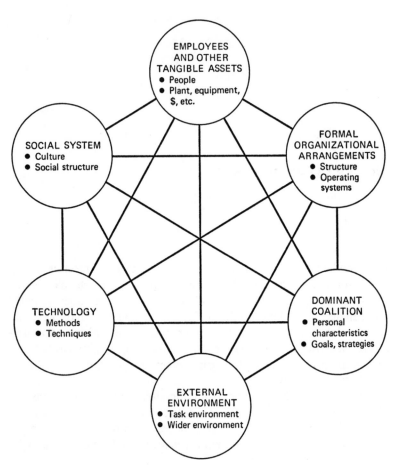

Fig. 4.1   The relationships among these six elements play a key role in shaping the moderate-run dynamics of the system.

elements in our model and has reached very similar conclusions.[2] This body of research offers evidence that when an organization's formal arrangements, employees and other assets, external environment, technology, internal social system, and dominant coalition have characteristics that "fit" together, that are "consistent" and "congruent," that are "coaligned," one tends also to find efficient matter/energy processes, effective information processes, and stability within a moderate time frame. If, however, the relationships among any of the six structural elements do not fit, or are nonaligned, one tends to find some inefficient matter/energy processes and ineffective decision-making processes emerging within a few months or a few years, and the situation tends to be unstable. Furthermore, the larger the nonalignment, or the number of nonalignments, the greater the number of inefficient and ineffective processes that tend to emerge, and the more unstable the situation tends to be in a moderate time frame.

What constitutes aligned and nonaligned relationships among any two or more structural elements is often intuitively obvious. For example, if the goals and strategies embraced by a firm's dominant coalition are based on inaccurate assumptions about the firm's task environment, then the dominant coalition and the external environment are obviously nonaligned. If the number of employees or the amount of tangible assets a firm has are not sufficient to take advantage of the economies of scale inherent in the organization's technologies, then the two elements are nonaligned. If the specialization called

---

2. I am referring to work such as J. Woodward, *Industrial Organization: Theory and Practice* (New York: Oxford University Press, 1965), C. Perrow, *Organizational Analysis: A Sociological View* (Belmont, Calif.: Wadsworth, 1970), E. D. Trist, G. W. Higgens, H. Murray, A. B. Pollock, *Organizational Choice* (London: Tavistock Publications, 1963), Chris Argyris, *Personality and Organization* (New York: Harper & Row, 1957), A. D. Chandler, Jr., *Strategy and Structure,* (Cambridge, Mass.: MIT Press, 1969), P. Lawrence and J. Lorsch, *Organization and Environment: Managing Differentiation and Integration,* (Boston: Harvard Business School, 1967), J. Lorsch and J. Morse, *Organizations and Their Members,* (New York: Harper & Row, 1974), and J. D. Thompson, *Organizations in Action* (New York: McGraw-Hill, 1967).

Table 4.1

Examples of the Important Relationships among the Six Structural Variables.

1. *External Environment—Dominant Coalition.* If the goals and strategy that are explicitly or implicitly being followed by the dominant coalition are based on incorrect assumptions about the external environment, inefficiencies will emerge and the situation will be unstable in the moderate run (and thus will probably change).

2. *Technology—Employees and Other Tangible Assets.* If the number of employees or the amount of tangible assets is much too small to take advantage of the economies of scale inherent in the organization's technologies, inefficiencies will emerge and the situation will be unstable in the moderate run.

3. *Dominant Coalition—Technology.* If the dominant coalition does not have members who are skilled in understanding the organization's main technologies, inefficiencies will emerge and the situation will be unstable in the moderate run.

4. *Formal Organizational Arrangements—Employees and Other Tangible Assets.* If the specialization called for in the formal organizational arrangements is inconsistent with either employee skills or the number of employees, inefficiencies will emerge and the situation will be unstable in the moderate run.

5. *Formal Organizational Arrangements—Social System.* If the relationships, rules, and goals spelled out by an organization's formal arrangements are significantly different from the relationships, norms, and values in its social system, inefficiencies will emerge and the situation will be unstable in the moderate run.

for in the formal organizational arrangements is inconsistent with either employee skills or the number of employees, than again there is a nonalignment (see Table 4.1).[3]

---

3. For a summary of some of the research findings regarding the association of four of the six structural elements (technology, employees and other assets, external environment, and formal arrangements) see J. Ford and J. Slocum, Jr., "Size, Technology, Environment, and the Structure of Organizations," *The Academy of Management Review* **2** (October 1977).

The key role that the relationships among the structural elements play in determining organizational dynamics in a moderate time frame can best be seen through a few examples of nonalignment:

- *Dominant Coalition—Social System.* When a college that specialized in a particular subject matter had an opening at the top, its trustees chose a new president from outside the school. Apparently unknown to the trustees was the fact that this person's training emphasized a point of view that was professionally at odds with values central to the college's culture. This nonalignment between the head of a new dominant coalition and the college's internal social system became apparent about two months after the new president took over when, at first subtly, the president and the faculty began to fight. After eight months, the warfare was open and seriously disrupting campus life. In the ninth month the president resigned.

- *Formal Organizational Arrangements—External Environment;* and *Employees and Other Tangible Assets—External Environment.* A large company had lived in a remarkably stable task environment for nearly twenty years. Within a two-year period during the early 1970s a great deal changed, however, and a significant part of that environment became very volatile. This change created a serious nonalignment between the new task environment and both the firm's formal organizational arrangements and its employees. The dominant coalition discovered that the very formal set of organizational arrangements that had served it well for a long time was now often a major impediment; the elaborate procedures and well-structured hierarchy that helped produce reliable processes to deal with a very routine set of environmental demands hindered the organization's efforts to cope with the new and nonroutine demands placed on it. It was also found that the type of employee and manager who had been hired and promoted for years had great difficulty dealing with the new realities; such employees found the ambiguity in the new situation threatening and reacted very defensively. As the organization's performance began to slide, its dominant coalition began to reorganize and hire a different type of person.

- *Technology—Dominant Coalition.* A moderate-sized corporation ran into difficulties in its efforts to transfer to the third generation of computers. These difficulties dragged on over a number of years until a vice president of operations was hired away from a major computer company. A post mortem of the affair, performed by a consulting firm, concluded that "the single biggest cause of the initial failures to successfully implement a third generation of computers was lack of computer expertise among top management and the board of directors" (that is, a nonalignment between the new technology and the dominant coalition).

- *Formal Organizational Arrangements—Employees and Other Tangible Assets.* A consumer products company grew very rapidly during the 1960s. The total number of its employees increased by a factor of three, while its formal organizational arrangements changed very little. At the end of this growth period, the firm was plagued with increasing problems that the dominant coalition traced to a nonalignment between its formal arrangements and the number of its employees. The formal arrangements, they found, were more appropriate for a firm half their size. On the basis of this conclusion, the president finally led an effort to restructure the firm.

- *Technology—Employees and Other Tangible Assets.* With the introduction of a new computer system in its accounting department, one corporation found that it required three hundred fewer employees there. It corrected this nonalignment by gradually transferring them elsewhere.

- *Social System—External Environment.* An organization with a long history and tradition found itself with an internal culture that was increasingly different from that found outside the firm. As this nonalignment grew, so did the organization's problems. For example, the organization had great difficulty dealing with the government and other externalities. On the brink of collapse, it was taken over by outsiders, who immediately began efforts to change the internal culture.

All of the previous examples share one common pattern, which tends to be characteristic of moderate-run organizational dynamics. Something causes a change that creates a significant nonalignment among two (or more) of the structural elements in our model. After a period of months or years, the states of those nonaligned elements change so that their relationships are aligned again (or almost aligned). During that period of time, problems tend to emerge and then go away, and a rather complex series of specific events (short-run cause-and-effect dynamics) occurs, which is related to the ultimate changes.

With an understanding only of short-run cause-and-effect dynamics, one could not anticipate the occurrence of this pattern in a specific organization, or predict exactly where it will take the organization. But with an understanding of what constitutes aligned versus nonaligned relationships, what tends to create nonalignments, and how they tend to correct themselves, one can both understand and predict the dynamics of an organization over a period of six months to six years.

PATTERNS IN THE CREATION AND CORRECTION OF NONALIGNMENTS

As the previous examples illustrate, a variety of factors lead to non-alignments. Perhaps the most common is a change of some sort in an organization's external environment, which then creates a nonalignment between that element and one or more of the other structural elements. Economic recessions, new technological developments, changes in consumer tastes, competitive product developments, and new federal and state legislation quite often create nonalignments for contemporary organizations.

For example, because of a number of changes in its external environment, a nonprofit organization once found itself increasingly dependent on the government for money and regulatory clearance. Its dominant coalition was not particularly oriented to or skilled at managing this dependence. As the organization began to face more and more problems related to the government, the key members of the dominant coalition resigned and were replaced with people who were better equipped to manage their new environment.

A second common cause of nonalignments is growth. Most modern organizations attempt to grow. They do so by expanding their task environments, developing new technologies, and adding employees and other assets. These growth-induced changes then often create nonalignments with other system elements. A significant increase in employees, for example, could easily create a nonalignment with the formal organizational arrangements that were designed to fit a smaller organization.

Management succession within the dominant coalition also often induces nonalignments. New leaders bring with them different skills and outlooks, a new set of relationships, and sometimes different goals for the organization. These changes can create nonalignments with any of an organization's existing structural elements. A new company president, for example, might have aspirations for growth that are not aligned with the firm's current task environment.

Finally, nonalignments are also often created by actions designed to correct nonalignments. The incorporation of a new technology, for example, might eliminate a nonalignment between the organization's technology and technological developments in the external environment, yet at the same time it might create a number of new nonalignments. The new technology might require a great deal of specialization in jobs of varying complexity. The current formal arrangements might call for less specialized and more similar jobs. Current employees might not have highly specialized skills. And the current social system might stress peer relationships and little status stratification. The new technology would then create nonalignments with all three of these elements.[4]

Once created, nonalignments tend to correct themselves by taking the path of least resistance. That is, they move toward a solution that requires a minimum use of energy. They generally do so by realigning around that element or those elements that are most difficult and expensive to change.

---

4. For a detailed description of a situation in the mining industry that is similar to the one described here, see E. D. Trist, G. W. Higgens, H. Murray, and A. B. Pollock, *Organizational Choice* (London: Tavistock Publications, 1963).

In the first example on page 41, where there is a nonalignment between a college's new president and its current culture, it is reasonable to assume that forcing this one individual to resign would require a smaller energy expenditure than making a change in the college's culture that would have been opposed by virtually the entire faculty. In the second example, where a major shift in a firm's task environment created a nonalignment with its formal arrangements and with some of its employees, it is also reasonable to assume that although the cost of changing employees and formal arrangements was high, it was significantly less than what would have been required to change the task environment. This is especially true because, for all practical purposes, some new aspects of this firm's task environment, such as an oil cartel, were impossible for the firm to change. In the third example, the costs associated with bringing in a new vice president of operations were obviously less than the potential costs associated with abandoning efforts to install third-generation computers in a company that relied heavily on computers. In the fourth example, reorganizing was certainly less expensive than trying to reduce the size of the company to what it had been five or ten years earlier. Virtually everyone with a stake in the organization would have resented a move to make it significantly smaller. The other examples fit this same pattern too.

While nonalignments all tend to correct themselves by means of the path of least resistance, the time they take to do so can vary widely. A number of factors can combine to correct a nonalignment in less than a month, or in more than a decade.

First of all, the more energy that is needed to correct the nonalignment, the more time it tends to take. Large and difficult changes tend to take much more time than small and easy changes. Laying off a small percentage of one's employees, for example, usually requires much less energy expenditure and will probably occur much faster than developing or incorporating a new major technology. Making a fundamental change in a firm's culture will usually require much more time and energy than adding a new formal system.

The speed of nonalignment correction is also usually very much a function of how much energy waste an organization's dominant coalition and its external environment are willing to tolerate. Nonalignments lead to inefficiencies and waste in matter/energy processes. If a firm's dominant coalition and its external environment are willing to allow such waste, and if the organization can afford this waste because of its favorable position vis-à-vis its environment, nonalignments will probably correct themselves slowly. At the extreme, it is possible under these circumstances for moderate to small nonalignments to go uncorrected for years and years.

For example, the leading corporation in an oligopolistic industry once took ten years to correct a nonalignment between a part of its technology and a new technological development in its environment. The firm received virtually no pressure from its environment to make the change more quickly. Because of the capital-intense nature of the industry, it was almost impossible for a new company to be formed to exploit the new technological development. The corporation in this case only had three competitors, and they were in no hurry to spend money to correct the nonalignment in their own firms. The industries' customers put little pressure on any of the corporations, and the government put none. At the same time, the corporation's dominant coalition was quite satisfied with this status quo. They could pass on the cost of the matter/energy waste created by the nonalignment to their customers in higher prices. And they probably did not want to risk bringing in a new technology that could then create nonalignments with other elements in their systems—including the dominant coalition. Under these circumstances, it is easy to see why the correction process moved so slowly.

SUMMARY AND DISCUSSION

System dynamics in a moderate-run time frame are significantly shaped by relationships among the six structural elements of the type shown in Table 4.1. An understanding of these aligned and nonaligned relationships, in conjunction with a knowledge of what tends to create nonalignments and how nonalignments tend to correct themselves, can help one both explain and predict organizational dynamics over a period of around six months to six years (see Table 4.2).

It is important to recognize, however, that knowledge of the relationships and patterns discussed in this chapter, while essential in

Table 4.2

Relevant Questions for Understanding or Predicting an Organization's Dynamics in a Moderate Time Frame

1 Are any of the following relationships out of alignment?
   a) External environment—dominant coalition
   b) External environment—formal arrangements
   c) External environment—employees and other tangible assets
   d) External environment—internal social system
   e) External environment—technology
   f) Dominant coalition—formal arrangements
   g) Dominant coalition—employees and other tangible assets
   h) Dominant coalition—internal social system
   i) Dominant coalition—technology
   j) Formal arrangements—employees and other tangible assets
   k) Formal arrangements—internal social system
   l) Formal arrangements—technology
   m) Employees and other tangible assets—internal social system
   n) Employees and other tangible assets—technology
   o) Social system—technology

2. What type of change created any identified nonalignments?

3. What might be the path of least resistance for correcting any identified nonalignments?

4. Given your understanding of the following, how long will it probably take for the nonalignments to correct themselves?
   a) The energy needed to correct any identified nonalignments
   b) The dominant coalition's willingness to allow waste
   c) The favorableness of the organization's position vis-à-vis its environment

helping one understand or predict organizational dynamics in a moderate time frame, is not sufficient to help one do the same in a short-run time frame. By itself, knowledge of a specific nonalignment does not guarantee that one can predict an organization's specific actions over the next seven days, for example.

Furthermore, just as knowledge of short-run dynamics was insufficient to predict behavior in a moderate-run time frame, knowledge of both short-run and moderate-run dynamics is insufficient to predict behavior in a long-run time frame. To chart an organization's probable behavior over ten or twenty years, one would have to do an impractical number of calculations involving (1) identifying upcoming nonalignments, (2) identifying the most probable way the organization will resolve each nonalignment, and (3) repeating stages (1) and (2) over and over again. To understand system dynamics in the long run, we need to consider yet another set of ideas.

5
LONG-RUN DYNAMICS

As contemporary organizations grow older, the states of their seven elements tend to become increasingly complex (with more internal differentiation and more internal relationships). More diverse types of people tend to be employed. More formal arrangements usually appear. A larger and more diverse task environment is developed. A more complex internal culture emerges. Additional technologies are incorporated. The size and complexity of the dominant coalition increase. But beyond this single pattern, one can find considerable diversity in the ways organizations evolve over long periods of time.

To understand why a particular organization evolves as it does over a period of six to sixty years, we need to consider what elements if any are acting as "driving forces," and what level of adaptability is built into the system.

DRIVING FORCES

The degrees of impact that the six structural elements in our model have on the seventh element of our model, the key processes, are seldom equal!. It is common for some of the elements to be more influential than others, and to remain so for significant periods of time. For example, in relatively young organizations that are run by an entrepreneur, the dominant coalition element (the entrepreneur) often tends to be much more influential than other elements. In high technology industries, the technology element is often the most influential. In very competitive, yet mature, industries, the external environment element is often more influential than others. In very old, well-established, institutionlike organizations, the internal social system and the formal organizational arrangements are often the most important elements. In both professional organizations and highly capital-intense industries, the employees and other assets element is often the most important.

Because of the nature of the interdependence among all seven of the elements in our model, whenever one or two elements are clearly more influential than the others, they become what might be called "driving forces" for the system.[1] Whatever direction they move in, the other elements "follow" in order to remain aligned.

Consider, for example, one small manufacturing company that evolved from 1960 to 1974 with the external environment acting as the driving force. In 1960, this firm utilized a single set of well-known technologies to manufacture a product line for a price-competitive geographical market. The firm had 150 employees, about $500,000 in equipment, and few formal arrangements. It was run by three brothers, and the atmosphere in the firm was like that of a family. In 1960 and 1961, the only significant change in the external environment was that the total market for the product line grew at 4 percent each year. In 1960 and 1961, the only significant change inside the company was that it grew 5 percent the first year and 4 percent the second. In 1962–1965, two important events occurred in the external environment. First, three new competitors started operations in this geographic market, which caused average delivery lead times to drop from six weeks to four weeks. Second, the total market grew 15 percent. Inside the firm, a number of things changed. People and equipment were added to keep up with the firm's 12-percent growth. A few formal procedures were added in response to the increased size. And the internal culture, which had never been concerned with speedy

---

1. I'm using the term "driving force" in a way similar to Richard Normann, *Management and Statesmanship* (Stockholm: Scandinavian Institutes for Administrative Research (SIAR), 1976).

deliveries, became so. Between 1966 and 1969, two more important changes occurred in the external environment. Once again, the total market grew, but in this period by 25 percent. In addition, one of the newer competing firms developed a new method (technology) for manufacturing a part of the product line. Inside the firm, major changes during this period included continued growth of personnel and equipment, the addition of a new layer of management in the formal structure to deal with the larger size, a corresponding increase in the number of levels in the informal social structure, the incorporation of the new technology, and a minor change in the formal organization of that part of the firm that used the new technology. And finally, between 1970 and 1974, the growth of the market leveled off; total growth during this five-year period was only 10 percent. Also, the real average price of their product lines, adjusted for inflation, dropped 20 percent. In response to these last two external changes, the firm added a number of cost control systems to its formal arrangements, developed a more cost-conscious culture, and hired a new purchasing manager to negotiate better raw material contracts. The firm also grew modestly during this period.

The evolution of a second firm during this same period of time was different in many ways. In this case, the firm's dominant coalition was the driving force. Although it also operated in a limited geographical area, it was smaller than the first firm in 1960, and was not in manufacturing; it offered a service. As such, it owned few physical assets. The company was run by four people, a president and three vice presidents, who were not related. They had a number of competitors in their geographic area, but not as many as the first firm. But most important, the four people who ran this company had an original concept of what kind of a company they wanted to create. This concept was developed by two of them while completing their education. Briefly, this concept called for hiring a slightly different type of employee than traditionally used by their competition, having those employees bring some new techniques to bear on the delivery of their service, and aiming this service at a set of customers who traditionally did not use their competitors' services. They created a "game plan" in 1959 that called for them essentially to create a new market, and to gain a dominant market share before their competitors could respond.

They anticipated that, if all went well, they would be ready to expand into new geographic areas by 1970.

Between 1960 and 1963, this firm began hiring the new type of employee, developing the new type of technology, redefining its task environment, and infusing its "concept" into its internal culture. These actions required a great deal of the dominant coalition's time and energy. Its revenues during this period increased modestly, but not as much as those of most of its competitors. Then, in 1964 and 1965, the firm began to experience some real success in creating a new market, and the dominant coalition focused their energies heavily on developing this market. In 1966, as they themselves describe events, "things took off." Revenues in 1966, 1967, 1968, and 1969 increased an average of 50 percent per year, and they could have increased even more if the company's leaders had allowed it. According to the company's president:

> We chose to manage our growth and not let it overwhelm us. We were not in any danger of losing significant market share, and we wanted to focus some of our efforts on the next stage of our development, which was expansion into new geographic regions.

Between 1966 and 1969, the firm added many new people and made numerous incremental additions to its formal arrangements. One of the vice presidents also spent considerable time during this period seeing that some of the important aspects of the culture they had developed in the early 1960s did not get lost because of the growth. In 1970, the firm opened an office in a different geographic area, and in 1973 it opened a second branch office. Armed with a clear strategy, the managers of these offices each began the process of developing a market and an organization to serve it. By 1974 the company was 2500-percent larger than it was in 1960, but it was not very different from what the original 1960 blueprint had planned for the mid-1970s.

While there clearly are similarities in the way both the service firm and the manufacturing firm evolved from 1960 to 1974, there also exist major differences, which are related to their driving forces. The direction in which the manufacturing firm evolved was primarily controlled by its external environment. The direction in which the service firm evolved was primarily controlled by members of its dominant coalition and their business strategy. An understanding of these facts helps us today to see why these firms changed as they did from 1960 to 1974. An understanding of these facts in 1960 could have helped us to predict the general direction and types of changes.

The concept of driving force is already implicitly used by some organization specialists and managers. But often because of their training, they assume that one of the system's elements is always the driving force, in all organizations. That is, they assume that the external environment or the formal organization or the technology provides the driving force for all organizations. Both the preceding examples and the dynamics inherent in our model suggest that this is not true. Although some elements undoubtedly provide the driving forces more often than others, any of the structural elements can be a driving force.[2]

THE NEED FOR ADAPTABILITY

A number of organization theorists have shown rather clearly that the key to an organization's long-run survival and prosperity lies in its ability to adapt to inevitable external and internal changes.[3] Within the context of our model, the logic of this observation can be expressed as follows:

1. Because some of the elements in the model are made up at least partially of physical and biological systems that naturally change over time, and because the elements are all interdependent such that changes in one tend to affect all the others, numerous changes in the system are *inevitable* over the long run.

2. Change can easily create nonalignments.

---

2. Some management writers have argued that while any element can be the driving force, the dominant coalition should always be the driving force. For example, see *Business Policy* by E. Learned, C. R. Christensen, K. Andrews, and W. Guth (Homewood, Ill.: Irwin, 1969).

3. For example, see E Schein, *Organizational Psychology* (Englèwood Cliffs, N.J.: Prentice-Hall, 1965) Chapter 7, and Warren Bennis, *Changing Organizations* (New York: McGraw-Hill, 1966), Chapter 1.

3. Nonalignments, when not corrected quickly, drain energy out of the system.

4. Therefore, unless an organization has an unlimited supply of surplus matter/energy, its ability to correct nonalignments (that is, to adapt) will directly affect its prosperity and survival over the long run.

Social science and managerial research suggest that an organization's ability to adapt to changes over the long run is primarily a function of the states of its structural elements. Those states can range anywhere on a continuum from highly constraining of organizational processes and hard to align with other structural elements, to very unconstraining and easy to align (see Table 5.1). Because the more constraining states make it difficult to adapt to changes in the short and moderate run, the organization will inevitably lose some energy while slowly adapting. And as this occurs again and again, or as the organization finds itself unable to make some needed changes, it can eventually drain off all its surplus energy and die. Therefore, the more an organization's structural elements look like those in the left-hand column of Table 5.1, the more problems one would predict it would face in the long run, and the greater the chances that it will not survive. The opposite is true when its elements look more like those in the right-hand column.

For example, an organization possessing a single technology that is rapidly becoming outdated and that requires large amounts of capital equipment will probably have much more difficulty adjusting successfully to new developments in its external environment than will an organization that possesses the more advanced technologies available for its products, services, and administrative systems, as well as a number of alternative technologies it might use in the future. If a competitor were to bring out a better product or service based on a new and different technology, the latter organization quite possibly could make some minor alterations in one of its advanced technologies and begin producing a comparable product or service within months. The former organization could just as easily find itself in the position of having to develop the new technology from scratch, a process that could be very time consuming and expensive, or of having to purchase the new technology at what could be an enormously high cost. It would also face the problem of selling its capital-intense assets that were based on the outmoded technology.

Likewise, an organization with an internal social system characterized by low trust, low power, low morale, little sense of shared purpose, and resistance to change, would probably have much greater difficulty adjusting to changes than an organization whose social system has norms, values, and shared purposes that are more supportive of adaptability. If such organizations were to find themselves having to make changes in their formal arrangements to align with a significant growth in number of employees and in other assets, for example, the former would probably require much more time and energy to create the change for a number of reasons. Because of the low trust, many employees would be suspicious of the dominant coalition's motives when a reorganization was suggested or announced and would probably look for ways to stop or undermine the change. Because of the low morale and low sense of shared purpose, the dominant coalition would probably have considerable difficulty trying to persuade employees to accept the changes. And because of the low power in the system, it is quite possible that neither the dominant coalition nor any employee group could completely impose its will on all the others, thus leading to a time-consuming stalemate.

In a similar way, an organization with rundown plant and equipment and underskilled employees would probably have more difficulty adapting to changes than an organization in which employees are highly skilled in diverse areas and in which equipment is in top-notch shape. Likewise, a firm with intelligently designed and flexible formal systems, a strong and talented dominant coalition, and a very supportive and benign external environment is clearly in a much better position to adapt to changes than a firm whose structural elements do not have such unconstraining and easy-to-align states.

To help clarify how organizations develop elements into highly adaptive or unadaptive states, and how that can affect organizational dynamics in the long run, consider the following example.

Table 5.1
Examples of Element States That Do and Do Not
Facilitate System Adaptation

	States That Are Highly Constraining And Hard to Align with, and Thus Do Not Facilitate Adaptation	*States That Are Not Highly Constraining, Are Easy to Align with, and Thus Facilitate Adaptation*
Technology	Organization possesses a single complex technology that is rapidly becoming outdated and that requires large amounts of capital for equipment.	Organization possesses the most advanced technologies for its products, services, and administrative systems along with a number of alternative technologies it might need in the future.
Social System	Key norms are not supportive of organizational flexibility and adaptability. Little trust found in relationships in social structure. Total power in the system is low. Morale is low. Little sense of shared purpose.	Key norms are supportive of organizational flexibility and adaptability. High trust found in relationships in the social structure. Total power in the system is high. Morale is high. High degree of shared purpose.
Tangible Assets	Plant and equipment in rundown state. Employees, especially middle management, are underskilled. Organization has some highly specialized equipment and human skills it doesn't need anymore.	Plant and equipment in top-notch shape. Employees, especially middle management, are highly skilled. Organization possesses equipment and people with skills that it doesn't need now but may need in the future.
Organizational Arrangements	Formal systems are not very sophisticated but are applied in great detail, uniformly across the organization.	Different kinds of formal systems exist for structuring, measuring, rewarding, selecting, and developing different types

	States That Are Highly Constraining And Hard to Align with, and Thus Do Not Facilitate Adaptation	States That Are Not Highly Constraining, Are Easy to Align with, and Thus Facilitate Adaptation
		of people working on different types of tasks. Formal systems also exist to monitor change in the organization and its environment and to change the formal systems accordingly.
Dominant Coalition	A small, homogeneous, reasonably untalented group with no effective leadership. All are about the same age.	A large, reasonably heterogeneous yet cohesive group of very talented people who work together well and have plenty of effective leadership. Members are different ages.
External Environment	The organization is very dependent on a large number of externalities, with little or no countervailing power.	The organization has only a limited number of strong dependencies, with a moderate amount of countervailing power over all dependencies.
	Demand for products and services is shrinking. Supplies are hard to get. Regulators behave with hostility and inconsistency.	Demand for products and services is growing. Supplies are plentiful. Regulators behave consistently and fairly.
	Public angry at the firm. Economy in bad shape. The political system isn't functioning well. Overall, the environment is hostile.	Public likes the organization. Economy is in good shape. Political system is functioning well. Overall, the environment is benevolent.

An Example of Adaptability Problems

Mr. Smith creates a
simple coaligned
system

In 1905 Mr. Smith, a high-school dropout, founded the Smith Corporation. On the basis of a new but relatively simple technology, he essentially created a product that didn't exist before and successfully sold it to a new and growing market. With no competition, Mr. Smith set up a simple manufacturing operation, hired workers, and expanded plant and number of employees as sales went up. He added a simple organizational structure at one point and the company grew with the expanding market. By 1910 his company had achieved considerable success.

Mr. Jones also creates a simple coaligned system.

In 1906, in a different part of the United States, Mr. Jones founded the Jones Corporation. Like Mr. Smith, he did not have much formal education but apparently did have some entrepreneurial talent. He too modified existing technology to create a new product line for an emerging market. He too hired workers and established a plant, and his firm grew. By 1910, he also had achieved considerable success. And the two companies, although in different businesses, looked very much alike.

Both companies grow, become more complex, but stay in coaligned states.

In 1920, both companies were larger and more complex, and both were still experiencing considerable prosperity. Profits were high, sales were growing, employees and customers expressed a high level of satisfaction, the plants hummed along efficiently, and so forth. Problems were hard to find in either company. In these respects the two companies still looked very similar.

The Jones Corporation's new complex-

But in other ways, the two companies looked very different. Mr. Jones had a small

ity was the result of element states that provided more resources and fewer constraints than the Smith Corporation's.

"development" group that was creating potential new products and methods for manufacturing them; Mr. Smith did not have a similar group. Mr. Jones had hired a "general manager" for his business (although he was still very active in the business himself); Mr. Smith did not. Mr. Jones's plant and equipment were maintained in top-notch shape; Mr. Smith's were not. Mr. Jones had a somewhat larger supervisory staff and encouraged them to take management courses at night school; Mr. Smith did not. Mr. Jones worked hard to create and keep, not just "good" morale, but very good morale among his employees. An oft-repeated motto of his was familiar to, and believed by, everyone: "Our future depends on our ability always to keep on our toes"; there was no such motto at Mr. Smith's company. Mr. Jones's general manager gradually introduced formal measurement, planning, and reward systems into the company that were considered by outsiders at the time as "very sophisticated for a small company"; Mr. Smith did not. One of Mr. Jones's salespeople, a "promotional genius," managed to create a continuous stream of favorable publicity for the firm; Mr. Smith got some publicity, but not much. Finally, Mr. Jones established a number of policies of "The customer is always right" variety that made his customers a bit more loyal than Mr. Smith's.

Changes caused non-alignments for both companies.

Between 1920 and 1925 both organizations continued to grow and make money, but they both began to feel "growing pains." Both were threatened with serious competition for the first time. Some of this competition had developed a slightly different method of making their standard product line at less cost.

The Jones Corpora-
tion makes changes,
bringing itself back
to coalignment.

The Jones Corpora-
tion continues to
maintain high re-
source/low con-
straint element
states.

The Smith Corpora-
tion, however, does
not take corrective
actions.

Changes occur once
again. Smith's com-
pany displays clear
performance prob-
lems.

Mr. Jones's company responded quickly to this new competition, bringing out a number of new products. As Mr. Jones began to feel less comfortable with the administration of the larger and more complex business, he turned more and more control over to his general manager. Among other things, during this period the general manager structurally reorganized twice to reflect new staff components of the business he was adding. He and Mr. Jones continued their efforts to keep their human and technological resources ahead of their need, to make themselves a respected institution, and so on.

The Smith Corporation did not really notice the competition at first. After nearly twenty years of success, no one in the firm took the competition very seriously. A few people recommended to Mr. Smith that he look into his competition's new technologies and that he rationalize the somewhat arbitrary formal structure that had grown up at the company. But he decided against both actions. He did not feel entirely comfortable with the new technology, and developing it looked expensive. He knew that if he rationalized the organizational structure he would very much upset two or three of his managers. Since profits and sales were still high, he decided not to take any risky actions and to just live with the problems that had begun to develop.

The Depression created problems for both companies, but of a different magnitude. Between 1929 and 1933, the Smith Corporation's sales and profits not only stopped growing, but dropped about 30 percent, whereas the Jones Corporation's sales and profits remained about constant. During this period Mr. Smith died, and Mr. Jones retired. Jones's general manager became president of the company. One of Smith's salespeople took over that organization.

The Jones Corporation adjusts to the changes, relying very much on the system's highly adaptable elements. Jones continues to prosper.

A combination of factors helped the Jones Corporation to adjust to the Depression: their reputation and customer loyalty, their fairly broad product line, their loyal work force, their planning systems (which helped them anticipate a number of important events), the competence of the general manager and his staff, and so on.

After 1933 the Jones Corporation started to grow again. Between 1933 and 1975 it increased ten times over, and today it is still a highly respected and successful company.

The Smith Corporation is unable to adjust to the changes; the nonaligned system performs poorly.

Between 1930 and 1938, the Smith Corporation's sales went up slightly, but its profits continued to slide. To boost sales, the new president agreed to a suggestion from his sales force to increase the options offered on their main product. This strategic move did improve sales (and sales commissions, which, among other things, reduced dissent in the sales force). But the action also created havoc within the firm's production and accounting departments, which were not organized to cope with what amounted to a fiftyfold increase in the number of products ordered and made. Other actions by the president also had a similar effect—temporary gains, but more problems.

And finally dies.

In 1939 and 1940, the Smith Corporation lost money. In late 1940, its bank refused further credit and the firm was liquidated.

In this example, both organizations achieved and maintained co-aligned systems during their early histories, and both achieved considerable success. But during this time one organization developed elements in states that were more facilitative to system adaptation. Mr. Smith's company developed elements that look more like those on the left-hand side of Table 5.1, while Mr. Jones's company developed its elements into states more like those on the right-hand side. Later, when the organizations were knocked out of coalignment by significant changes (competition, new technologies, management succession), Jones, Inc. generally was able to cope with these changes, re-creating a coaligned system. Smith, Inc. was not able to do so. Indeed, the Smith Corporation's elements were so constraining and its inability to adapt to changes so large that the company eventually died.

This example clearly demonstrates a number of the important characteristics of organizational adaptability, some of which most managers and organization specialists recognize, and some of which they do not. It is obvious to most that creating adaptive structural elements requires intelligent expenditures of matter/energy. Without the application of time, effort, and resources, the structural elements tend to become more and more constraining and less and less alignable over time.[4] But it is not obvious to most that adaptability is a function of *all* the structural elements. Some managers tend to think that a good market position, or good leadership, is the key to adaptability, while some organization specialists seem to think that the internal social system, the technology, or the formal arrangements are the key to adaptability.

In subsequent chapters, when we are considering some of the more important managerial and organizational development implications of our model, we will explore further why it is that some organizations, like Mr. Jones's, are able to successfully develop, when others are not.

SUMMARY AND DISCUSSION

In the long run, organizational dynamics are shaped primarily by the system's driving force (or forces) and the adaptability of its structural elements. The driving force determines the general direction in which the system will evolve, and the adaptability of the structural elements

---

4. This tendency has been called, among other things, organizational entropy. See Chapter 3 in Chris Argyris's *Intervention Theory and Method* (Reading, Mass.: Addison-Wesley, 1970).

Table 5.2

Relevant Questions for Understanding or Predicting an Organization's Dynamics over Long Periods of Time

1. Does the organization have one (or more) driving force? If yes, what element (or elements) provides the driving force? Why is it that that element (or elements) provides the driving force?

2. In what direction is the driving force moving? What does that imply over the long run if all the other elements follow in order to stay coaligned?

3. How facilitative of adaptation are each of the structural elements:
   a) The dominant coalition
   b) The formal arrangements
   c) Employees and other tangible assets
   d) The internal social system
   e) The technology
   f) The external environment

4. Is the organization actively trying to invest resources so as to make the structural elements more adaptive? What does this imply regarding the organization's prosperity and survival in the long run?

helps determine its prosperity and its chances of survival (see Table 5.2).

While very important in determining dynamics in the long run, the system's adaptability and driving forces do not necessarily help one to understand or predict dynamics in shorter periods of time. For example, an organization that has three or four of its structural elements in states that are very unsupportive of adaption will undoubtedly experience difficulties in the long run; but the organization may or may not experience problems in the moderate run depending on whether the elements are coaligned or not. To understand moderate or short-run dynamics, factors such as the alignment of elements and cause-and-effect relationships must be considered.

The essence of the model has now been entirely presented (see Table 5.3). The model describes a very dynamic system that is neither biological nor cybernetic, although it has aspects of both. It focuses

Table 5.3

System Dynamics: A Summary

Time Frame	Key Factors in Shaping the System's Dynamics
Short run (a few days to a few months)	Two types of cause-and-effect dynamics in conjunction with the current states of the seven elements.
Moderate run (a few months to a few years)	The relationships—aligned or nonaligned—among the structural elements, in conjunction with the short-run factors.
Long run (a few years to a few decades)	The "driving force" and the adaptability of the structural elements, in conjunction with the other moderate- and short-run factors.

on both structure and process, and does so for all types of organizations. It contains economic, psychological, sociological, and managerial variables. It contains relationships of cause and effect as well as of association. If focuses on short- and long-run development. It offers an integrative perspective based on fifty years of research on formal organizations.

To help you better appreciate the implications of this model, we focus next on the issue of organizational effectiveness. Chapter 6 identifies what the model can tell us about organizational effectiveness, and what causes organizations to develop in effective and ineffective ways.

6
SOME IMPLICATIONS FOR
ORGANIZATIONAL EFFECTIVENESS

The model developed in the last four chapters is essentially descriptive; it does not tell us what types of organizational dynamics or what system states are "good" or "bad." However, if one supplies criteria for "goodness," one can then deduce from the model both what types of system states are "good" or "bad," and what type of dynamics might lead an organization toward or away from such states. The reader has no doubt already done so to some degree while reading these chapters. In this chapter, such criteria will be explicitly supplied, and the implications regarding organizational effectiveness and ineffectiveness will be explored.

A CRITERION FOR
ORGANIZATIONAL EFFECTIVENESS

Most people, though not all, would label an organization "effective" in a short-run time frame if the organization's key processes displayed a high level of matter/energy efficiency and decision-making effectiveness. In such a case, the organization would be wasting a minimum of raw materials, of human energy, and of machine potential. It would also be handling information in a rational way. It would not, for example, be diverting employee energy into hostile actions on or off the job, or systematically ignoring important information it needs in its decision making.

Most people would probably judge an organization effective in a moderate-run time frame if they felt it was capable of maintaining its short-run effectiveness over the moderate run. That is, they would rate an organization effective if they felt it could maintain the key processes element in an efficient and effective state over a moderate time frame. In terms of our model, they are describing a system state in which the structural elements are all aligned—a state of coalignment.

Most people define effectiveness in a long-run time frame as an organization's capacity to adapt quickly to the inevitable changes that occur; that is, to move quickly into a new state of coalignment when a change has caused it to go into a state of nonalignment. As we saw in Chapter 5, an organization's ability to adapt is a function of the adaptability of its structural elements. Therefore, in terms of the model, an effective organization from a long-run point of view is one in which most of its structural elements are in highly adaptive states.

Overall, therefore, we would deduce that a highly effective organization, in terms of our model, is one in which the key processes are in an efficient and effective state, while the six structural elements are coaligned and are in highly adaptive states (see Fig. 6.1).

This conclusion regarding organizational effectiveness may seem obvious to some readers. Nevertheless, a close examination will reveal that it is *different* from the beliefs held by many managers and organization specialists today. Many of these people, explicitly or implicitly, think that organizational effectiveness is associated either with certain "best" states—like good leadership, a dominant market position, loyal employees, a high level of current profitability—or with a fit among certain organizational and situational components—such as between the organizational structure and the company's strategy, or between the organization and its environment. The model suggests that all of these positions are right, to some extent, and wrong also, in being too limited. Specifically:

1. Those who believe in "contingency" or "fit" models are correct when that say that moderate-run effectiveness is associated with a fit among system elements, not with any specific element states.

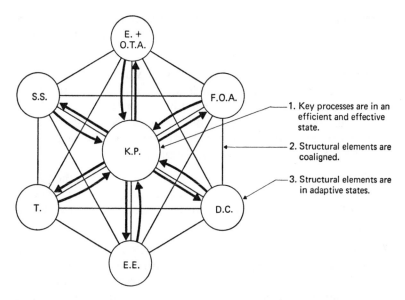

Fig. 6.1 The characteristics of a highly effective organization.

2. Those who believe in "one-best-way" models are correct when they say that long-run effectiveness is associated with certain "best" states of each element (that is, states that facilitate adaptation), or when they say that short-run effectiveness is associated with a single best state in the key processes (that is, the state displaying matter/energy efficiency and effective information processing).

3. But at the same time, contingency models are wrong when they assert that fit leads to long-run effectiveness. As we have seen in the last chapter, an organization can be in a system state of coalignment and therefore be performing well in the short to moderate run, and yet it may fail in the long run because most of its elements are not in highly adaptive states.

4. Some contingency models are also wrong when they assert that effectiveness is a function of a fit between fewer than all six of the

elements in our model (for example, between just formal arrangements and the external environment, or between just the social system and the technology).

5. The one-best-way models are also wrong when they suggest that an organization can achieve moderate-run effectiveness simply by getting one or more of the elements into their "best" states. If the overall system is significantly out of coalignment, the organization may not only perform poorly in the moderate run, it may perish as a result of that poor performance.

6. Some of the one-best-way models are also wrong when they assert that long-run effectiveness is always dependent on the adaptability of only one or two specific structural elements, such as the social system, and not on others.

7. And finally, neither the contingency models nor many of the one-best-way models are particularly sensitive to short-run dynamics, and therefore to the problems of either correcting a nonalignment or pushing an element into a more adaptive and less constraining state. Contingency or fit models often seem to imply that once you have identified the misfit, the problem of ineffectiveness is practically solved. Similarly, few one-best-way models provide realistic details concerning how to create their best states. In this sense, both types of model are inadequate.

In general, therefore, our model suggests that many conventional views of what is associated with organizational effectiveness are narrow and limited. They all overlook certain correlates of effectiveness. In doing so, they can easily mislead managers and organization specialists in their efforts to improve organizational functioning.

ACHIEVING ORGANIZATIONAL EFFECTIVENESS

Achieving a high level of organizational effectiveness, one can deduce from our model, requires either an enormous amount of good fortune, or more likely, a little good fortune combined with an ongoing series of very well made decisions, especially regarding resource allocation. Specifically, to attain a high level of effectiveness, an organization must use its limited resources successfully in three ways: (1) to make sure, in the short run, that the key organizational processes stay in an effective and efficient state; (2) to create or maintain a coalignment among the six structural elements; and (3) to push its structural elements into, or maintain them in, highly adaptive states. To do so requires that the organization be sensitive to these needs, that it monitor all three aspects of organizational effectiveness, and that it judiciously and intelligently allocate its surplus resources to these three ends.

The model does not, however, provide any simple mechanical formula for making these resource allocation decisions. It only suggests that these decisions can be made more successfully if one focuses on all three aspects of effectiveness, and if one uses the model to test the implications of alternative improvement interventions on short-, medium-, and long-run effectiveness. Numerous examples of exactly how the model can be used as such are found in the next chapter.

A careful examination of our model also suggests that achieving a high level of effectiveness, at least under contemporary conditions, should be very difficult. For example, one can deduce from our model at least three broad reasons why organizations might develop ineffectively. These reasons relate to (1) the complexity of the system; (2) the potential for conflict between what is best for the organization and what is best for individuals; and (3) the dysfunctions caused by having too much surplus energy in the system, or by not having enough surplus. By examining each of these factors, we can gain considerable extra insight into the issue of organizational effectiveness.

Organizational Effectiveness Problems Caused by Complexity

When one considers the amount of relevant information (from the seven different elements) and the uncertainties involved (especially as you consider three different time periods), it quickly becomes clear that one of the barriers to organizational effectiveness is the complexity of the situations in which modern organizations find themselves, and the complexity of the decisions that have to be made by these organizations.

At any moment, for example, an organization with some unexpended energy—let us say in the liquid form of money—has to make a number of very difficult decisions regarding what to do with that money. Imagine, for example, a manager who has only $10,000 in discretionary funds available for the next few months; he is trying to decide which of three projects deserves the funds. In project number 1, he would give the $10,000 as a bonus to his engineering vice president, who, he feels, has been instrumental in creating and maintaining a high quality product development process under difficult conditions, but who seems to be letting up recently. The $10,000, he thinks, would reflect the company's recognition and appreciation; furthermore, it would probably help motivate the vice president to keep the effectiveness of the development process (and the organization's short-run effectiveness) from slipping. In project number 2, he would hire a consultant to study how the company should reorganize now that it has doubled its size in five years and gone into a new business. He knows that at some point the current structure must be modified to fit the new realities (and to maintain the firm's effectiveness in the moderate run). In project number 3, he would take advantage of an opportunity he recently identified. A marketing manager working for one of his competitors had let him know that she was interested in exploring a move. The president thinks very highly of this person, and has one opening in middle management in his marketing department. With the $10,000 added to the marketing department's salary budget, the company could afford to hire this person (and contribute to the firm's long-run effectiveness by improving the adaptability of the employees and other assets element). In choosing one of these three options, the president could easily consider thousands of factors—and still it would be a difficult decision because of the complexity of the situation.

One can also easily imagine a slightly different situation in which a manager has just decided to use the surplus to increase the adaptability of his organization. With that decision made he then faces alternatives such as the following:

1. The extra resource can be invested in improving organizational technologies and in searching for new ones (and their associated products or services).

2. It can be invested in tangible assets such as plant and equipment.

3. It can be invested in upgrading employees' skills.

4. It can be invested in improving formal systems, designing ones that will be needed in the future, and planning.

5. It can be invested in the social system—in creating high productivity and high flexibility norms, in improving trust in relationships, in increasing a shared sense of organizational purpose, and so on.

6. It can be invested in upgrading the dominant coalition—in bringing in a broader range of skills, in improving its ability to work together (team building), and so on.

7. It can be invested in programs aimed at creating a more favorable task environment, by such means as finding new suppliers, lobbying to increase tariffs, or increasing consumer awareness of their products.

8. It can be invested in improving the organization's public image in its wider environment.

9. It can simply be left liquid in a bank account.

People who have been successful in general management jobs for a number of years tend to fully recognize this complexity. Younger managers and organizational specialists often do not.

Organizational Effectiveness Problems
Caused by Conflicts of Interests

Our model also suggests that, under certain conditions, it is possible for the dominant coalition to have interests that are significantly different from the organization's. In pursuing their own interests, such leaders would then systematically create organizations that were less than highly effective. For example:

1. The dominant coalition of the leading organization of its kind in New England diverted hundreds of millions of dollars of profits during the 1930s, 1940s, and 1950s into the hands of their own families (through dividends) and invested very little in the business. By the late

1960s, the firm, while still very large, was no longer profitable and did a poor job of serving its customers and employees. A new dominant coalition moved in and has made some, but not a great deal of, progress in the last seven years in its attempt to improve the financial condition of this atrophied organization.

2. The members of the dominant coalition in one major corporation each owned well over $1 million in the company's stock. In the early 1970s, that stock dropped to one-third of its 1970 high. There were weeks in which the dominant coalition members each "lost" (on paper) $50,000. Under those circumstances it was difficult for them to focus on their real jobs. Instead, it was very tempting to take whatever short-run measures might quickly boost the stock price. And they occasionally did. As a result, the dominant coalition managed to force up the stock price (which was then sold as they retired) while undermining the organization's effectiveness.

In less dramatic ways, many managers often systematically develop their organizations in ineffective ways mainly because they are rewarded almost entirely for short-run performance. With praise, career opportunity, and money allotted to them on the basis of short-term achievements, they spend far too much of their personal and discretionary resources trying to keep current processes effective and efficient, too little of their time and other resources trying to create or maintain a coalignment, and far too little effort trying to create adaptive element states. Some managers are masters at creating an impressive short-run performance in this way. They appear to be successful because they move on to other jobs after one or two years, leaving the longer-run problem they have created for someone else.

Organizational Effectiveness Problems
Caused by Too Much or Too Little Surplus

Our model also suggests, as others have observed before, that a third factor that can undermine organizational effectiveness is, ironically, too much success. The following example is typical of companies that initially achieve a high level of success only to slide into decline in later years.

Frank Worben and his successor, George Thompson, led the Worben Manufacturing Company into a new market area before anyone else, capturing an overwhelming market share. As a result, between 1925 and 1950, WMC grew from a company with annual sales of $4 million to one with sales of $250 million.

With the retirement of George Thompson in 1946, a nephew of the original entrepreneur, Tom Worben, became president. Most people who knew him said that Tom was significantly less capable than either George Thompson or his uncle.

During the early 1950s a number of new competitors entered WMC's markets. The company did not react in any planned way to these developments. Some insiders claim that a few of the new competitors were simply not noticed for five years or more.

In 1960, WMC's sales grew by only 5 percent for the first time in nearly thirty-five years. Its net income grew by 1 percent. Tom Worben and his management group began to initiate a number of remedial actions, including diversifying into a few new product lines. In retrospect, most of their decisions look fairly uninformed. None of their actions helped the situation much.

In 1968, WMC lost money for the first time in its history. Its bank stepped in and demanded that the board of directors appoint a new president and management team. After a power struggle, a new board and a new dominant coalition emerged. This new group initiated major changes in the organization during 1970 and 1971. Financial analysts who were close to the situation claim that these changes saved the company from bankruptcy.

An extremely successful organization, like WMC, that far surpasses all rivals for a significant period of time, usually develops a certain dominant position in its task environment that, in a sense, decouples it from the pressures and demands of that environment. It also often develops an overly self-confident management. Not wanting to believe that their good fortune, which often far exceeds their original ambitions, is attributable to chance, the key managers in such an organization begin to believe what others often tell them—that they are brilliant. In such an organization, it becomes hard to believe that one needs to worry seriously about the future. In the absence of tension, the dominant coalition and others tend to slow down the processes that use energy to maintain or increase the adaptability of the system's elements. Over a period of time, the adaptability of elements within the organization goes down, but without causing visible problems; the strong position vis-à-vis its environment allows the organization to make mistakes, to develop some nonalignments, to correct them slowly, and yet not suffer from these mistakes in any significant or obvious ways—in the short run. This apparent good fortune reinforces the whims of an overconfident management, which continues to ignore both the decreasingly adaptable elements and the growing nonalignments. This in turn usually leads to a crisis, at which point some of these organizations actually perish.

Almost the opposite situation, too little surplus matter/energy, can also lead to ineffective organizational development. Without a minimum surplus, an organization will simply be unable to invest in interventions that make its elements more adaptive or that maintain it in a state of coalignment.

There are typically three types of situations in which one finds such underfinanced organizations. Young entrepreneurs sometimes cannot get the external financing they need for an adequate matter/energy surplus. Divisions of large companies are sometimes used as "cash cows"; they are treated as a source of funds rather than a place to invest more money. And public organizations are sometimes created, given a mandate, and then not funded at a level appropriate for carrying out that mandate, much less for building an effective organization.

SUMMARY AND DISCUSSION

Applying commonly held criteria of what constitutes organizational effectiveness to our model, we find it describing a system state in which the organizational processes are operating efficiently and effectively, the structural elements are in a state of coalignment, and most of the elements are maintained in highly adaptive states. Creating organizational effectiveness thus requires investing matter/energy sur-

Table 6.1

Relevant Questions for Determining the Level of an Organization's Effectiveness and the Forces That Limit Greater Effectiveness

---

1. How efficient and effective are the key organizational processes?

2. How close is the organization to a state of coalignment?

3. How facilitative of adaptation is each of its structural elements?

4. How large are the barriers to improving the organization's effectiveness? That is,
   a) How complex is the organizational system?
   b) Is there an important conflict of interest between the organization and its dominant coalition?
   c) Has the organization had too much or too little surplus?

---

plus in the achievement of this state. Doing this, the model suggests, is made difficult by numerous barriers related to complexity, conflicts of interest, and too much or too little success (see Table 6.1).

One of the important implications of this model is that both managers and organization specialists need a good understanding of and a healthy respect for the complexity of modern organizations and the many barriers that exist to developing them and managing them effectively. Current models and theories of effectiveness all too often understate, ignore, or underestimate the complexity and the barriers.

7
USING THE MODEL

The model presented in this book is not meant to replace more specialized models, frameworks, and theories used by managers or organizational specialists. Nor is it meant to provide specific answers to standard questions, as does, for example, a linear programming model. Instead it is designed to supplement existing models by raising important questions that other models might ignore, by providing a more powerful basis for understanding and predicting organizational dynamics, and by helping one to think broadly about organizational improvement issues.

The purpose of this final chapter is to help the reader see more explicitly how the model presented in the previous chapters can be of use. This chapter will focus on how the model can help both managers and organization specialists diagnose organizational effectiveness and make organizational improvement interventions. In addition, it will discuss how the model can be of special use to organizational staff or consulting specialists in establishing effective helping relationships with managers.

DIAGNOSING AN ORGANIZATION'S EFFECTIVENESS LEVEL

The model can help both managers and organization specialists diagnose an organization's effectiveness level primarily by alerting them to all the facets of effectiveness that need to be considered. Specifically, it suggests that they carefully examine the following:

1. The current efficiency and effectiveness of information and matter/energy processes;

2. The relationships among the six structural elements (are they co-aligned?)

3. The adaptivity level of the structural elements.

Many managers and organization specialists tend to ignore one or more of these aspects of effectiveness. The case of a large service firm, as told by its marketing vice president, is typical in this regard:

> If you had asked me in 1960 how effective our organization was, I would have said, without hesitation, that it's very effective. We had just finished building the kind of sales force we thought we needed to sell the new service we introduced in 1958. By 1960, that service accounted for 85 percent of our sales, which overall were up 15 percent from 1959—a new high. Profits in 1960 set a new high also. Everything looked great.
>
> In retrospect, it is easy to see a big mistake we made. In judging how effective our organization was, we did not consider questions of adaptability. We thought only in terms of short-term profitability, and in terms of strategic fit—that is, did our service fit market needs, and did we have an organization that was capable of selling and delivering that service? Had we also been thinking in terms of adaptability, we would have rated that aspect of our effectiveness as low. The sales force we created, for example, was very inflexible. People in it were selected, trained, and rewarded with only one consideration in mind—selling that one service. Had we recognized this back in 1960, I'm sure we could have avoided many of the problems we have encountered in the past eight years.

In 1969, this firm introduced a number of new services in response to changing industry conditions. For the next five years, the company found itself constantly struggling to get its sales force to sell the new services properly. Because of significant growth during the 1960s, the firm was no longer in a position where it could economically hire a new sales force that was better suited to the new conditions (which is essentially what it did during the late 1950s). They had to rely mostly on their existing sales force, which was not very able to adapt. In 1974 alone, company executives estimated that their sales were 25 percent lower than they should have been, while their profits were 30 percent lower, due to this problem.

While the adaptability aspect of effectiveness is probably most often ignored, managers and organization specialists will sometimes ignore other aspects of effectiveness too. For example:

1. The head of a moderate-sized high technology company focused her energies almost entirely on "developing an organization for the future." She wanted the "best" employees, the "best" customers, the "best" technologies, and so forth. In 1972, a major new product was introduced that was incompatible with short-run market needs. This precipitated a financial crisis that very nearly bankrupted the company.

2. An organization specialist worked very closely with the head of one small service company in the late 1960s. The two of them implemented a number of organization improvement techniques aimed at resolving conflicts and improving relationships in the internal social system, at developing the interpersonal and supervising skills of their managerial employees, and at designing a better performance appraisal system. They were largely successful in their efforts, and even received some favorable publicity as a result. But in the early 1970s, the firm's sales suddenly dropped 70 percent in two years, and this company also nearly went into bankruptcy. In a post mortem of the affair, one analyst concluded that "the company just did not fit the business they were in. They did well initially because of good economic conditions, an enthusiastic staff, and luck. When their luck ran out, and the economy got tough, they collapsed."

In each of these cases, a knowledge of the model in this book would not necessarily have guaranteed success, but it would have alerted the people involved to those aspects of effectiveness that they were ignoring, and that subsequently caused them problems. In addition, as we shall see next, it could have helped them to identify and implement interventions designed to avoid those problems.

MAKING ORGANIZATIONAL IMPROVEMENT INTERVENTIONS

The model can help managers and specialists in their selection, implementation, and evaluation of organizational improvement interventions in two important ways. First, it can help them diagnose exactly what is causing and what has led to whatever problems they have identified. Second, it can provide a rational basis for identifying feasible interventions, and for assessing their probable impact if implemented (see Appendix, especially Part II).

For example, this model helped a production manager to identify the error in his diagnosis of a "personality" problem. The manager was in charge of a number of production units, including final quality control. He had received an increasing number of complaints about product quality from the company's customer service department. Upon investigating the situation, he concluded that the supervisor in charge of quality control did not have the kind of personality that could effectively supervise the twelve individual inspectors. On the verge of making some personnel changes, he was introduced to our model. Intrigued by it, he spent some time gathering additional information and rethinking his original diagnosis. As a result, he learned that over the past six months a set of informal relationships and norms had developed within the quality control group that were very "anti-management." Because of the informal leadership of two inspectors who had been hired within the preceding year, the quality control group had become close knit and very resistant to outside managerial influence. When their supervisor had tried to intervene to maintain and improve their work habits, he was not only resisted, but was attacked in subtle and unsubtle ways. It was because of some of these attacks that the production manager had originally concluded that the supervisor did not have the personality to be a good supervisor. On the basis of this new diagnosis, the manager decided not to transfer or demote the quality control supervisor, but to work with him to select and implement interventions into the work group's social system. He did so, and over the next six months the quality control problems gradually disappeared.

In another case, our model helped a moderate-sized manufacturing company to understand some complex dynamics and problems that they alone, and previously another organization consultant, had been unsuccessful at diagnosing. In this case, the first consultant identified the problem as a deep set of conflicts between top and middle management. Top management felt that numerous people in middle management were not completely competent in their roles. Middle management, however, felt that the company's inability to achieve its objectives was caused by the attitudes and decisions of top management. Working from that diagnosis, the first consultant used an intergroup development technique that briefly improved the relations between the two management groups. Nevertheless, the company's performance did not improve, and relations began to deteriorate again.

A second consultant, using the model in this book, helped them diagnose the situation quite differently. He found that because of a series of seemingly insignificant decisions over a period of ten years, the company's technology and task environment had both become considerably more diverse and complex—much more than either top or middle management explicitly recognized. While the company had been selling largely to one type of customer in 1964, in 1974 it was selling to five types of customers who were very different. While the company used essentially one basic type of technology to design and manufacture its products in 1964, by 1974 it was using four types. These changes produced some large nonalignments with other system elements, such as the formal arrangements. The nonalignments eventually created a variety of performance problems that both top and middle management tried to solve. But their efforts were largely in vain, and after a while considerable frustration built up in both groups that then led to finger-pointing and scapegoating.

Using our model, the consultant found that the reason they were so unsuccessful in correcting the nonalignments was that their efforts were all directed at making rather small changes in formal arrangements and personnel. The consultant concluded that these changes were just not fundamental enough to eliminate the large nonalignments. He concluded that eliminating the nonalignment between the formal arrangements and both the technology and task environment would require either (1) reorganizing from a functional organization into four product line divisions, or (2) eliminating a number of customers, technologies, and products so they would fit with minor or no changes in the current structure.

Only when the second consultant was able to help the troubled company understand his diagnosis did they succeed in beginning to eliminate problems that had plagued them for years. After explicitly deciding that they did not have the resources to build and staff a four-division structure, they began to focus on the company's business—its technology and task environment—with the aid of a strategic consultant that the organization consultant recommended. After top management had made changes to reduce the diversity and complexity of their businesses, the organization consultant helped them to use some organizational improvement tools to make some small changes in their social system, employees and other assets, and formal arrangements so as to fit the newly defined technology and task environment. Within a year after these changes were in place, the company began to accomplish its objectives for the first time in years, and relations between top and middle management improved dramatically.

In yet another situation, an organization specialist was asked by a corporation to help it identify why it seemed to be having problems with its newer employees, who often became disappointed within twelve months and left the company. The consultant talked with both managers and younger employees and concluded that the basic problem was that the company did not utilize any managerial process to help new people get up to speed quickly and effectively. Working with managers who supervised new employees and with key personnel representatives, she helped them design and implement a process that started during recruiting, and ended after a twelfth-month performance review. During the six months the consultant continued to work with the company, the new process worked well; new employee morale went up and turnover went down. But six months after the consultant had left, the process had essentially disappeared and the original problems began to reappear.

Had this consultant been using our model, she would have recognized that her intervention would create helpful changes only in the short run. Specifically, a test of her intervention with the model would have shown the following:

1. Intervening directly into the information and matter/energy processes would be feasible. The states of the other six structural elements would not prevent the emergence of a new process.

2. However, the process would be unstable after the consultant left unless changes were also made in two of the other structural elements; the social system and the formal arrangements. The formal performance evaluation system made no attempt to measure or reward supervisors for their effective involvement in this new process. Furthermore, there was a fairly strong set of shared beliefs among the supervisors' bosses (middle managers) that giving special attention to new employees was somehow wrong. Basically, they believed in the sink or swim approach. The model suggests that both of these factors would work to undermine the newly created process.

At a later date, a manager within this company used our model and concluded that three interventions were necessary: one into the processes, one into the formal arrangements, and one into the social system. He then proceeded with the aid of an internal organization specialist to select and design improvement techniques that could help implement three such interventions. And the positive changes, this time, remained stable.

Another case in which a manager probably could have avoided making an ineffective intervention involves a manager in a large multinational firm who decided to select and implement a management training program. His purpose was to upgrade the quality of the company's management and make them more adaptable to future contingencies. He spent considerable time examining various management training programs and then designing an elaborate sequence of programs to be implemented over a period of ten years. However, six months after the first training session, the entire program was set aside by the company's president. To this day, five years later, it has not been started up again.

Had the manager in this case tested the short-run impact of implementing an elaborate training intervention before investing much money in it, the outcome might have been different. Had he done so, he would have anticipated that:

1. The company's industry was about to go into a difficult period.

2. The company's president would soon (within twelve months) be under extreme pressures to maintain some level of profits.

3. In light of his past behavior, the company's president would probably respond by cutting most expenditures that were not necessary in the short run, including management training.

Having seen that this intervention, as he originally conceived it, would not work, he could have looked for and tested other alternatives. There probably was at least one feasible alternative besides abandoning the training idea. That intervention should have *begun* by focusing on the company's president, with the objective of gaining his understanding and commitment to management training. It is quite conceivable that if the president had understood and been committed to management training, he would have cut expenditures elsewhere and allowed the training program to continue.

The theme running through all these cases is that our model provides a better basis for making difficult decisions about organizational improvement interventions than the ad hoc models used by many managers and organization specialists. It provides a more comprehensive world view. It helps managers and organization specialists to think more clearly about complex and dynamic organizational issues. And it helps them to be more effective in their work.

ESTABLISHING AN EFFECTIVE HELPING RELATIONSHIP

From the moment an organization specialist comes into contact with a client or potential client, he or she is forced to make important decisions. How much and what type of information should I try to obtain from the client now? Where do I probe, and where should I just accept the client's responses? Does this sound like a situation where I can be of help? How can I best answer the client's questions? What should the next step be? How can I convince the client to take the next step? These initial decisions are particularly important because they quickly determine the nature of the consultant-client relationship. Good answers to these questions can help establish effective relationships that are beneficial to managers, their organizations, and the specialists. Poor answers can lead to ineffective relationships or, perhaps even more often, no relationship.

Without an adequate model of organizational dynamics, such as the one presented in this book, organization specialists are forced to make important initial decisions based on either a more limited model, or their past experiences. Sometimes these past experiences are in a broad enough spectrum of situations that the person has developed a fairly comprehensive model. More often they are not. Consider the following example:

> A Ph.D. trained staff organization specialist in a large United States corporation contacted a division manager about the possibility of using some type of survey feedback exercise to help improve the effectiveness of the division's decision-making process. The division manager was intrigued with the idea, and for the first fifteen minutes of their first meeting was both friendly and enthusiastic. The division manager asked the staff person what this exercise would cost the division. The staff specialist assured him that his services and those of his staff would be paid for out of corporate funds and therefore would cost the division nothing. The division manager looked puzzled. "But what about the cost in time to my employees?" the division manager asked. The specialist replied that it would be impossible to improve an organization's health without some investment of time and energy on the part of the organization's employees. The division manager paused, and in a more reserved manner asked the specialist when he would suggest that the initial questionnaires be sent out; he suggested early May. The division manager pointed out that during the first three weeks of May his marketing people would be involved in the two biggest trade shows of the year, and the plant people would be tied up in a maintenance shutdown where all

managerial people work twelve-hour days. The division manager then asked if the OD person had ever worked with any companies in their industry before. The specialist said no, but tried to assure the division manager that he had worked with similar organizations, and that all organizations are similar in many important ways. Continuing in a reserved manner, the division manager asked what risks he would be taking if he went ahead with this program. The specialist said that while no situations are risk free, the risks here would be very small. "Specifically what are they?" the division manager asked. The specialist paused and then gave a long answer that focused on the risks of not having an effective organization. "How healthy or unhealthy is the division?" the division manager asked. The specialist replied that he didn't have enough information to judge, but that in light of the division's lack of sales growth that year, and the strike it had had at one of its plants, there was probably lots of room for improvement in employee relationships and in decision-making processes. (Although the division manager said nothing at this time, he was possibly wondering if the specialist knew that the division was one of only three companies in its entire industry that had not seen a decline in sales that year, and that the division was the only company in its industry that had not had all its plants shut down by a strike for a two-week period the previous September.) The division manager politely ended this meeting and promised to get back to the staff OD person soon after he had "talked the idea over" with some of his managers. The division manager never did get back to the staff specialist. When the specialist called the division manager, he was politely told that the managers had argued convincingly that they had higher priorities now.

The staff specialist in this case was not an incompetent individual. On the contrary, he had a reasonably impressive track record; in the past five years he had worked as an internal organizational consultant and had completed three large and successful projects in three different divisions. He was unquestionably very bright, and was respected by his fellow professionals. However, his implicit organizational model did not pay much attention to economic, technological, industry, and market variables. And that limitation was directly related to his failure to establish an effective relationship with that one division manager. Knowing both the division and the specialist's staff, I think I can safely say that his staff clearly had tools that could have helped the division. They never got another chance.

Had the specialist in this case been using our model, he might have approached that whole situation differently. For example, prior to this meeting, the staff consultant phoned a few people he knew and asked them about the division manager he was about to meet. That was the extent of his homework. Had he been thinking more in terms of our model, he might have taken just a bit more time both to call people and to look for written information on the types of questions raised in the tables in Chapter 2. That is, he would have tried to learn something about the business the division was in (the external environment and the technology), their organization (tangible assets, formal organization arrangements, and the social system), and their operations (organizational processes), in addition to the information on the division manager (the key person in the dominant coalition).

With this information in hand, the staff consultant would have been in a much better position to establish a relationship of trust and confidence with the division manager. When a consultant says something that obviously does not take into account something the client sees as important and relevant, it cannot help but undermine the client's faith in the consultant. And if the consultant does that repeatedly, as our staff consultant did, it will often simply force the client to conclude that the consultant cannot be of help.

The preliminary information that the model guides one toward can also be valuable in helping organizational specialists tentatively decide whether they can be of any help. A few hours of preliminary information gathering will sometimes show, for example, that the organization has so hopelessly deteriorated that it is probably beyond help, or that the dominant coalition (the client) has interests that are so in conflict with the organization's that it is impossible for someone to serve both.

Had the staff consultant been thinking in terms of our model at the meeting itself, he could have been more aware of and sensitive to the frame of reference of the division general manager. The model suggests, for example, that if he is going to establish a rational relationship and contract with the manager, the specialist must help the manager answer questions like the following:

1. What volume of resources am I committing with this decision to work with this consultant? Are there obviously better alternatives for using these resources?

2. What are the short-run implications of this decision? What dynamics am I setting into motion? What about the moderate-run implications? The long-run implications?

3. What are the risks involved to my position in the dominant coalition? What are my personal stakes in this decision?

And finally, had the staff consultant been thinking more in terms of our model, he would not even have considered recommending some type of intervention—*any* type of intervention— until he was confident in his diagnosis of the situation. He would have fully recognized the dangers in blindly intervening with some "general purpose" solution or approach.

The usefulness of the model can be seen even more clearly if we contrast what the organization specialist actually did in the preceding case with another case in which the consultant did utilize our model. This second scenario began when the personnel vice president of a moderate-sized corporation called this organization specialist and asked him to help design and implement a fifteen to twenty session training program for middle managers in the company's manufacturing department. The consultant suggested they get together to talk about it and asked to meet and chat with the company's president and the manufacturing vice president (probably key people in the dominant coalition). Before these meetings, the consultant talked to another person who had worked with the company and learned, among other things, that (1) it was a family-owned business, and the president controlled over 50 percent of the stock, (2) a large part of their success was due to the firm's flexibility and efficiency in manufacturing, and (3) recently a national union had been trying to organize the plant. While traveling to the meeting the consultant read a description of the company's industry that his secretary had located. Upon arrival, he talked first to the personnel vice president, then to the manufacturing vice president, and then to the two vice presidents and the president together (the president arranged it that way). In these conversations the consultant spent about half the time working to gain these people's trust by demonstrating an appreciation for their situation, and about half the time asking questions to get more information. He learned quickly that turnover in manufacturing had increased recently to 40 percent in the work force and to 20 percent among the managers. He also learned that none of the three executives he had talked to had a good answer as to why the turnover was occurring, and, moreover, that the three clients all had slightly different answers. He ended his visit with them with the following remarks:

1. No, I won't help you design and implement a management training program—at least not right now. I simply do not have enough evidence that that will solve the turnover and union problems that you are concerned about. What is needed, it seems to me, is a much better understanding of exactly what factors are creating these problems. Then we can decide whether we need management training or something else.

2. To get a better understanding of the situation we can proceed in a number of ways. At a minimum, I would like to talk to twenty or so people in manufacturing. If you have any strong feelings regarding exactly how to proceed, let me know within the next few weeks. I will think about it too, and send you either a specific recommendation or a set of alternatives within three weeks.

3. Here is the name of another company and its president that I have helped in a similar way. It would probably be a good idea if you called him.

Within three weeks the consultant sent the company a recommendation regarding how to start. Four weeks later the personnel vice president called and asked the consultant when he could begin.

In the same way that the model can provide a powerful basis for helping managers to select and implement organizational improvement interventions, it can provide organizational consultants with additional support in establishing effective helping relationships. At a time when the ever-growing number of organizational improvement tools are probably being severely underutilized by managers, such support is very much needed.

SUMMARY

The model of organizational dynamics described in this book offers managers and organizational specialists a way of thinking that can help them more effectively diagnose an organization's health, make improvement interventions, and develop effective adviser-client relationships. It can both supplement more specialized models and replace less powerful ad hoc models. While hardly a panacea for organizational ills, it has clearly demonstrated an ability to improve organizational effectiveness.

In an age in which we have become more and more dependent on formal organizations for the goods, services, and salaries that support our whole society, anybody who can improve the effectiveness of those organizations can have a significant impact on the quality of the lives of billions of individuals. Behavioral science and other types of organizational improvement techniques provide one source of hope for the future. The model presented in this book offers managers and organization specialists a way to utilize those tools more effectively.

APPENDIX
A Summary of Questions
to Guide Diagnosis and Intervention

I Diagnosis

A. The External Environment

1. Considering the organization's current products or services, what other organizations, groups, or important people constitute its task environment? That is, who are the relevant potential suppliers, customers or clients, regulators, competitors, and so on?

2. What are the key characteristics of the various entities in the task environment in terms of size, objectives or desires, stability, capabilities, technologies used, attitudes about the organization, and so on?

3. If the organization is in a clearly definable industry, and thus has competitors, why is it that some of its competitors are more successful than others? What are the key success factors in this industry?

4. With whom does the organization currently interact? How dependent is it on each of those external elements? In each case, what is the basis of that dependence? How much countervailing power does the organization have? What is the basis of that power?

5. What are the most important characteristics of the organization's outer environment? What are the current economic, political, legal, technological, and social trends of importance?

6. What major changes have occurred (if any) in the above factors in the past decade?

7. Will any aspect of this element probably change in a significant way in the foreseeable future?

B. The Dominant Coalition

1. Who is in the organization's dominant coalition? Describe each of these people in terms of personal skills, attitudes, motives or desires, assumptions about how organizations should be organized and run, and so on.

2. What are the relationships among the members of the coalition? How cohesive a group is it? Who has the most power?

3. What goals and plans for the organization does the group share?

4. How powerful is this group vis-à-vis others in the organization? What is the basis of this power?

5. What major changes have occurred in the dominant coalition over the past decade? Are more significant changes probable in the forseeable future?

C. The Formal Organization Arrangements

1. What is the organization's formal structure? Draw a chart showing jobs, departmental groupings, a reporting hierarchy, responsibilities, and authorities. Also list any committees, teams, task forces, regular meetings, and so on.

2. What types of formal procedures exist for the following:

a) Allocating resources

b) Controlling financial resources

c) Measuring individual or unit performance

d) Selecting people

e) Training people

f) Rewarding people

3. How have these formal arrangements changed in the past decade? Are more significant changes probable in the foreseeable future?

D. Employees and Other Tangible Assets

1. What assets does the organization own, lease, or employ? Catalogue all the organization's owned or leased tangible assets, including land, buildings, equipment, suppliers, inventories, cash, and securities. Also catalogue the number and types of people employed.

2. What condition are the nonhuman assets in? How well have they been maintained? How liquid are they? What price could each obtain if converted quickly into cash?

3. What are the backgrounds of different employee groups? What are their skills and abilities? How do they feel about the organization? What are their expectations regarding the organization and their future?

4. How has all this changed? Are more significant changes probable in the foreseeable future?

E. The Internal Social System

1. What organizationally relevant norms exist among most employees or subgroups of employees? For example, what norms, if any, exist regarding how hard people should work and how conflicts among people should be resolved?

2. What organizationally relevant values exist among most employees or within subgroups of employees? Do any of those values relate to what the organization should be or should achieve?

3. What types of relationships exist among employees, especially regarding trust, level of cooperation, and power?

4. What types of relationships exist among natural subgroups in the organization, again regarding levels of cooperation, trust, and power?

5. How has the internal social system changed in the past decade? Are more significant changes probable in the foreseeable future?

F. The Organization's Technology

1. What is the organization's "core technology" (that method used in creating its primary goods or services)? Describe the technology—for example, if the organization is a manufacturing firm, does it use a job shop, large batch, mass production, or process technology? How complex is it? What kind of assets are needed to use it?

2. What other technologies does the organization use to produce goods or services? Describe them.

3. What technologies does the organization use to administer itself? Describe these too.

4. How has this technology changed in the past decade? Are more significant changes probable in the foreseeable future?

G. The Key Organizational Processes

1. What supplies (matter/energy resources) does the organization import? In what volume? At what cost?

2. Exactly how are these resources transported and converted into goods or services?

3. How are the goods or services disposed of? In what volume?

4. What other processes exist to manage the processes in questions 1–3 and to plan for the future?

5. On the basis of answers to questions 1–4, what are the key decisions made in the organization?

6. How are these decisions made? That is,
   a) What individual or group makes these decisions?
   b) How exactly does the individual or group make these decisions?
   c) What information is used?
   d) Where does that information come from?

7. How have these processes changed in the past decade? Are more significant changes probable in the foreseeable future?

H. Overall Effectiveness

   1. How efficient and effective are the key organizational processes?

   2. How close is the organization to a state of coalignment?

   3. How facilitative of adaptation are the structural elements?

   4. Can you think of any changes in the foreseeable future that will alter your answers to the previous three questions? If yes, what are the changes, and what effect will they probably have?

I. Source of Ineffectiveness

   1. Which specific processes, if any, are not very efficient or effective (now and in the foreseeable future)?

   2. How much out of alignment, if at all, are each of the following relationships (now and in the foreseeable future):
      a) External environment—dominant coalition
      b) External environment—formal arrangements
      c) External environment—employees and other tangible assets
      d) External environment—internal social system

e) External environment—technology

f) Dominant coalition—formal arrangements

g) Dominant coalition—employees and other tangible assets

h) Dominant coalition—internal social system

i) Dominant coalition—technology

j) Formal arrangements—employees and other tangible assets

k) Formal arrangements—internal social system

l) Formal arangements—technology

m) Employees and other tangible assets—internal social system

n) Employees and other tangible assets—technology

o) Social system—technology

3. How unadaptive are each of the structural elements (now and in the foreseeable future):

a) The dominant coalition

b) The formal arrangements

c) Employees and other tangible assets

d) The internal social system

e) The technology

f) The external environment

J. Dynamics Leading to Ineffectiveness

1. How much, and in what ways, are each of the following elements contributing to the emergence of each ineffective or inefficient process you have identified?

a) The external environment

b) The dominant coalition

c) The formal organizational arrangements

d) Employees and other tangible assets

      e) The internal social system

      f) The technology

2. How are any nonalignments you have identified contributing to the emergence of these ineffective or inefficient processes?

3. What historical circumstances (changes) created the non-alignments?

4. How, if at all, have the nonadaptive elements you have identified contributed to the existence of these nonalignments?

5. What historical circumstances led to the development of these nonadaptive elements?

6. How, if at all, has the organization's driving force or forces contributed to the development of nonalignments or nonadaptive elements?

7. What circumstances led whatever element (or elements) is the driving force to emerge as such?

K. Barriers to Improvement

1. How large are the barriers to improving the organization's effectiveness? That is,

      a) How complex is the organizational system in this case?

      b) Is there an important conflict of interest between the organization and its dominant coalition?

      c) Has the organization had too much or too little surplus, leading to the development of hopelessly unadaptive elements?

II. Intervention

A. Alternatives

1. In light of your diagnoses, what interventions might be appropriate? Note: It is best at this point to consider as wide

a range of interventions and organizational improvement tools as possible.

2. What is the approximate cost of each intervention? Be sure to take into account all direct and indirect expenses.

3 In light of your answers to the previous questions, and in light of your command of resources—power and money—in the organization, which of the alternatives are really feasible?

B. Probable Impact (answer the following questions for each feasible alternative)

1. If implemented in the immediate future, what would probably happen? That is,

a) Given your understanding of short-run cause and effect, how would each change immediately affect the key processes (if it were a structural change) or each structural element (if it were a process change)?

b) What would most likely happen next? And then next? Trace the interaction of processes to structures to processes until the system achieves an equilibrium and stops changing, or at least for a period of time of three or four months.

2. In light of your answer to the previous question, will the intervention do any of the following:

a) Successfully eliminate some source of ineffectiveness

b) Create any new nonalignments, or reduce the adaptability of any of the elements, or alter the system's driving force (or forces)

c) If you answered the previous question yes, then what will be the probable consequences of these unwanted changes? That is,

i) What might be the path of least resistance for correcting any new nonalignments?

    ii)   Given your understanding of the energy needed to correct any new nonalignments, the dominant coalition's willingness to allow waste, and the favorableness of the organization's position vis-à-vis its environment, how long will it probably take for the nonalignments to correct themselves?

   iii)   What does any reduced adaptability imply for the organization's prosperity and survival in the long run?

   iv)   What does any change in the driving force imply, over the long run, if other elements follow it to try to stay coaligned?

3. If the intervention were implemented in six months, in a year, or a few years from now, would that significantly affect your answers to questions 1 and 2 above? If yes, how?

C. Choice

1. Do any of the feasible interventions, given your previous answers, seem to produce results that justify their cost?

2. If yes, which of those interventions, or which groups of those interventions, seem to make the most sense in light of all of this analysis?